Southwold Street Names

a speculative history

by

Jenny Hursell

Published in 2011 by Jenny Hursell

Design by Holm Oak Publishing
24 Church View, Holton, Halesworth, Suffolk IP19 8PB
www.holmoakpublishing.co.uk

Printed by Southwold Press

A CIP catalogue record for this book is available from
the British Library

ISBN 9780953340651

Acknowledgements

My thanks to Southwold Town Council for access to the Gooding Collection and for permission to use photographs in the Town Hall; to the Suffolk Record Office for access to the Southwold Borough Archives; to the Southwold Museum & Historical Society and to David Lee in particular who checked that I had made no major historical blunders; to John "Dusso" Winter and Ronnie Waters for their local knowledge and for not screaming when I asked yet another obscure question; to Anthea Marriner and the Fox Trust for information about Tony Fox; to Doug Palmer for the use of family photographs; to John "Wiggy" Goldsmith for the use of a photograph in his collection; to John Lavery for use of two of his photographs; to St. Edmund's Church; and to Judy and Fred Butter for permission to take a photograph of their house, Beacon Cottage. Especial thanks are due to Ann Green for manipulating my text and illustrations into a printable form and for kicking me over the finishing line, and to Michael Mayhew at the Southwold Press for his equanimity when I discovered a major omission at the eleventh hour.

Bibliography

Becker, M. Janet (ed) *Story of Southwold*, F. Jenkins, 1948
Bottomley, A.F., *A Short History of the Borough of Southwold*, Southwold Corporation 1974
Bottomley, A.F., (ed) The Southwold Diary of James Maggs 1818-1876 Suffolk Records Society 1983
Clegg, Rebecca & Stephen (eds) *Southwold: Portraits of an English Seaside Town,* Phillimore & Co Ltd 1999
Lawrence, Rachel, *Southwold River: Georgian Life in the Blyth Valley,* Suffolk Books 1999
Macksey, Major-General P.J., *The Southwold Guns* (2nd ed 1965)
Storrs, Constance, *Jacobean Pilgrims from England, early C12th to late C15th* (1994)
Wake, R., *Southwold and its Vicinity, Ancient & Modern*, Yarmouth, F. Skill 1839

Opposite:

Map of Southwold (not to scale)

Reproduced by kind permission of the cartographer

and copyright holder, Wilfrid George

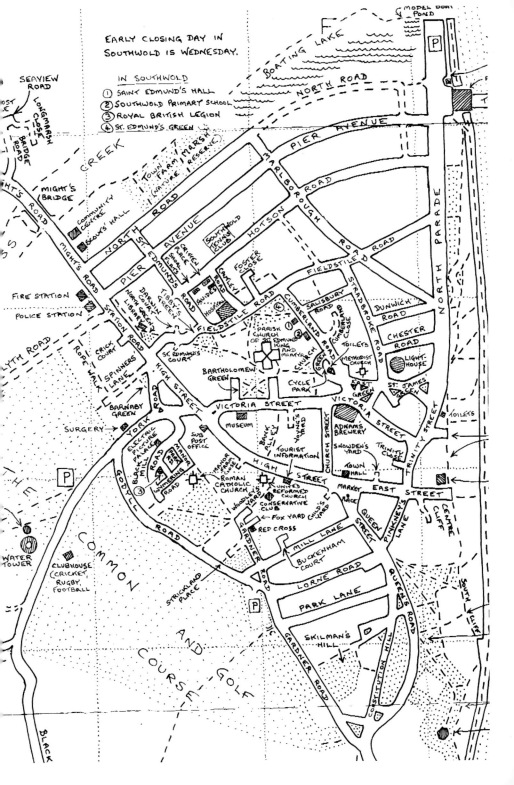

Introduction

Towns and villages other than Milton Keynes or Brasilia grew organically expanding from a huddle of private dwellings around a central area to larger settlements also comprising public buildings like meeting houses and churches. People popped next door for a convivial bowl of gruel or to complain about young Aethelstan chucking bones over the fence, and paths formed. As more people trooped to the church to thank God for the herring, say, or to the meeting house to complain about the herring rent, longer, well-beaten paths built up on what are called desire lines and in the course of time these became the street patterns known today.

There was no need for these routes to be named because the communities were so small: everyone knew where everyone lived and the man from DHL was not calling; but as settlements developed there came a time when naming their thoroughfares became useful. They were not usually very imaginative, often merely directional, based on compass points or the town or village they were heading towards or the building they were leading to.

If a community was walled its street names often included the word 'gate' e.g. Northgate - the road leading to the gate in the northern wall. Southwold was not fortified so it has no 'gates'. It does not have many directional street names either and the ones it appears to have like North Road and Church Street are not as straightforward as they seem.

Unlike neighbouring Reydon it has no Wangford, Halesworth or Lowestoft Road because, of course, there is only one road out of Southwold and to name it after one village rather than another would have been seen as undiplomatic. Anyway, Southwold has never been in the habit of naming its streets after other towns; it prefers people to places as you will see.

In the course of this book I refer many times to a handful of maps and other books. The significant maps are one which purports to show Southwold in the period 1670-1725; the so-called Ablett map of 1801 which was traced from the original in the mid 1800s; and the map which appeared in Robert Wake's *Southwold and its Vicinity* in 1839.

There are also numerous references to *The Southwold Diary of James Maggs 1818-1876* edited by A.F. Bottomley 1983, to various chapters in *Southwold: Portraits of an English Seaside Town* edited by Rebecca and Stephen Clegg and to *A Short History of the Borough of Southwold* by A.F. Bottomley. I also refer on several occasions to a seminal meeting of the Southwold Borough Council held on 25th May 1911 which was called specifically to name streets. Would that the Council was still asked to name new streets and that that privilege was not gifted to individuals.

BANK ALLEY

It's daft, people say, calling Bank Alley, Bank Alley. Woodley's Yard should be Bank Alley and Bank Alley should be Parson's Cut or Church Passage, but, of course, there has not always been a cash machine in Woodley's Yard. There are, in fact, indications from the 1801 map drawn by Thomas Ablett, and other documents, that Bank Alley was indeed once called Church Passage or Church Path.

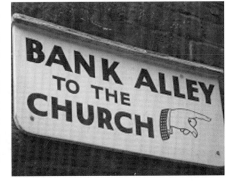

The late 17th century map shows it as a footpath crossing fields, with no houses on it, but conveniently providing a short cut from the vicarage, then on the High Street roughly where The Manor House is, and the church, so a church path it was.

In the early 1800s when James Maggs of Maggs Diary fame was the local postmaster, the main Southwold Post Office was in the High Street on the corner of the alley, the property now called Rutland House, but by 1839 the map in Robert Wake's *Southwold and its Vicinity* shows that that building had become a bank. In his text he refers to this bank in his usual understated way : "We cannot omit to express the universal acknowledgement on behalf of the public, of the accommodation and advantage offered by a branch of the Norwich Crown Bank . . . the business is now conducted in an elegant, modern-built mansion, situated in the centre of the High Street."

By 1839 there were buildings in the alley immediately behind the High Street properties but the row of cottages towards Victoria Street did not appear until later in the century, St Edmund's Cottage, as the plaque on it testifies, being built in 1883. Bank Alley benefits from the fine blue engineering paving bricks or setts forming its surface. It benefits less from the wheelie bins which now stand sentry in it.

BARNABY GREEN

Cottages on Barnaby Green, 1901

I hope the residents of Barnaby Green will forgive me for saying so but their green is a bit of an oddity is it not? It's not like Southwold's other greens: it's tiny, it's hedged and it is not clear if you can sit on it. Scant need for 'No Ball Games' signs here; but it was not always thus. In the 16th and 17th centuries The Common was fringed by small farms and the 1670-1725 map shows that the most northerly of these was called Barnaby's Farm. It was situated behind the triangular block where the King's Head is and adjacent to Forest Farm, an association recalled by Forest Cottage now on that site. There is a Barnaby Lodge on Godyll Road whose back garden at least was almost certainly part of Barnaby's Farm.

When I started thinking about the derivation of Barnaby I thought it could be a corruption of Barnabas as in the saint (and Southwold does have the residential home St Barnabas on The Common not so far away) or linked with bishy barnabee, the old East Anglian name for ladybird. Having dismissed that as pure fancy I recently learned firstly that bishy barnabee is believed to be derived from the 16th century Bishop Edmund Bonner, a vicious persecutor of heretics; and secondly that a 1799 lease relating to the King's Head refers to the adjacent green as Bonnier's Green, which is all very interesting but the early map pre-dates that. There is anyway evidence from the local records of Barnabys in the area and no doubt at some point they farmed there. The Southwold marriage registers record a Robert Barneby (sic) of Warley in Essex marrying Sarah Andrews of this parish on 12th November 1796.

The map referred to above pre-dates that as well, of course; perhaps the lad was coming home to marry his childhood sweetheart. Sadly the only other reference in the Southwold records is to the death in 1799 of a Sarah Barnaby aged 2. However, there are several references in the Reydon registers. James Barnaby, a labourer, and his wife, Rachel, had four children baptized there between 1816 and 1826 the youngest of whom was George, a labourer like his dad, who between 1852 and 1859 had three sons with his wife, Susan, all baptised in St Margaret's, Reydon.

Wake's 1839 map shows Barnaby Green covering the

area from the former Common Gate where York Road meets Godyll Road through to the High Street either side of the King's Head block. Maggs notes that from 1815 a former Powder Magazine (an ammunition store) converted into a prison house stood on Barnaby Green before being sold in 1837 to a Mr Goff of Wrentham and that in 1842 Mr Fulcher purchased houses upon Barnaby Green from Mr George Downing for £115. The 1894 Municipal Roll lists 21 people living on Barnaby Green and it was not until 1913 that the usurping York Road was named and Barnaby Green shrank to its present size.

BARTHOLOMEW GREEN

In the 1489 Charter Henry VII confirmed Southwold's right to hold the fair which became Trinity Fair (and then Charter Fair) and granted a further right to hold a second fair on 24th August. This was called Bartholomew Fair and was held on the open ground in front of St Edmund's. The more famous Bartholomew Fair in London, immortalised by Ben Jonson, was held annually from the 12th century to 1850. It was originally called the Cloth Fair but as it was held on the eve of Saint Bartholomew's feast day, the day itself and the day after, the saint's name gradually took over from the original name particularly when its trade became more general. Mediaeval fairs were more like markets and Bartholomew was an appropriate saint to name a fair after being the patron saint of butchers, corn chandlers, cobblers, leatherworkers and salt and cheese makers amongst others.

Bartholomew Green was also the site of the town's Guildhall, a two - storey brick building which formed part of the wall between the church-yard and the green. Here, on the upper floor the great and the good met for civic and legal sessions whilst the ground floor was used by the not so great but probably equally as good, serving as an almshouse and also the Corporation's store. Records indicate that this building was thatched in 1662 and repaired again four years later. By 1724, however, it was apparently in such a state that the Town Assembly agreed that it should be pulled down, which it was, but not until 1815. That year was also the last time the traditional Bartholomew Fair took place until its revival by John Bennett in 1996.

There were no buildings shown on the green in the 17th century map apart from one on the corner with the current Victoria Street on the south-west side (see photo below), but by

Bartholomew Green, present day

Wake's time there were properties along both that and the opposite side, albeit not reaching as far as the church walls.

Bartholomew Green suffered on the night of 15th May 1943 when a bomb destroyed homes there as well as Hollyhock Square behind them. The bombed houses were rebuilt as flats.

Although no longer the civic centre of the town the green is still an important focus as the main route to St Edmund's and the site of the War Memorial where crowds gather on Remembrance Day and Remembrance Sunday.

Bartholomew Green, circa 1870

BLACK MILL ROAD

The Black Mill was built in 1798 and stood on The Common where St Barnabas now is. It was brought from Yarmouth by the Council who had tired of repairing the Town or White Mill (see Mill Lane) which had been built on an exposed site in the middle of The Common. Catching the wind was a good idea but catching too much, as anyone who has played sport on The Common could vouch was inevitable, was not.

Old maps indicate that there had been a mill near the St Barnabas site prior to 1798, within the grounds of a farm called Common Farm. The Council perhaps judged that this would be a less vulnerable spot for the new town mill and to some degree this was so; the mill survived there for almost a century but it did need regular repairs. Fortunately the cost of these did not fall on the town for long. Initially the mill was let to a Mr Peregrine Edwards for £10 a year on the basis that the Council would maintain it provided that he ground corn for the poor at the price of one shilling per coom, a coom being a back-breaking sackful. After five years, however, Mr Edwards bought the mill outright and worked it for a further 33 years. It passed through various hands thereafter but in an increasingly parlous state: it lost a pair of sails in 1860, caught fire in 1863 and was finally demolished in 1894. Its presence on that part of The Common is recalled in the names of the houses there: Mill Villa, Old Mill and Mill House.

Black Mill, 1865

I have been unable to determine when the road was formed and named. Maps even as late as 1884 fail to show even a footpath following the route of Black Mill Road. Perhaps there was a track between the Forest and Barnaby Farms and Common Farm or perhaps the powers that be when making a permanent road there wanted to record the historical connection. Certainly the road was in existence prior to 1911 because the proposals considered by the Council that May included the suggestion that the roadway between Black Mill Road and Wymering Road be called Eversley Road. However, the first reference to Black Mill Road in the municipal or electoral rolls was in 1914 but given that even now there are only two residential properties recorded there this is hardly surprising.

BLACKSHORE

The whole northern bank of the Blyth at the harbour is often erroneously called Blackshore, not least by the current harbour authority, Waveney District Council, but in fact Blackshore is strictly the area where Blackshore Cottages, the Harbour Inn and the Sailing Club are situated. Blackshore Quay has been in existence at least since the early 18th century. It certainly predates the Reydon Quay which was built in 1737 with its own alehouse and which led to Blackshore and Southwold losing trade. The Reydon Quay was advantageous to the landowners of the Blyth Valley who used the river for importing coal and exporting corn. It was cheaper to transport goods by boat rather than over land so using the Reydon Quay, which was several miles further inland than the Blackshore Quay, saved them money. Southwold was not amused and as was its wont raised its objections nationally, but it lost. The tables have since been turned, of course. Echoes of Reydon Quay's importance remain in the name Quay Lane and Quay House but the alehouse has become a private residence whilst Blackshore still bustles with boats and imbibers at the Harbour Inn.

Blackshore as depicted in an 1860 painting

11

BLYTH ROAD

Blyth Road is presumably so named because it heads towards the river Blyth although both Carnsey Road and Ferry Road could have been so called on that basis. It has changed very little over the centuries apart from the relatively brief interlude of the railway. The 17th century map shows it as a track heading towards the river between the Common Field and sheep and cow pasture and that, apart from the 50 yards or so at the Station Road end which the County Council has adopted as highway, and the unaesthetic but useful sewage plant, scrap yard and so on which lurk down there now, is what it remains. It was not in fact until 1970 when the Borough Council built the houses on the northern side of the roadway that it was graced with a name. Prior to that Stanley Cottages were listed under Station Road in the electoral roll.

During the 50 years of the railway (1879-1929) the station buildings occupied the site of the present Police and Fire Stations and one of the chestnut trees which were a feature of the station platform remains in the corner of the Police Station yard.

Of course the truth about Blyth Road is that it is not a road at all and this has given rise to no end of hassle and complaint. As far as Suffolk County Council is concerned Blyth Road is no more than a footpath and despite the fact that some authority in the dim and distant past gave people the right to drive along it in order to access the sewage plant and the amenity site etc, the County has refused to maintain it as a road. The result has been potholes, broken sumps and a string of complaints from people from as far away as Halesworth. And who was blamed? Southwold, of course. Not fair! But then things looked up.

After far too much buck-passing the owners of the sites generating the most traffic and the most wear to the path's surface agreed to pay not only for a decent surface but to maintain it in a reasonable condition thereafter. For such mercies much thanks. Unfortunately, however, the new surface laid in the summer of 2010 at a cost of £40,000 soon deteriorated. The County Council agreed that the contractors had done a poor job and called them back to repair the roadway at their expense, and then after all that the County decided to close the amenity site altogether in 2011. Quite what the future of the road is I do not know, but at least its name will remain the same.

Blyth Road

CARNSEY ROAD

This road does not exist officially. It is not on the electoral roll because there are no houses on it and it does not appear thus named on any map. It is the stretch between the junction of York Road and Godyll Road, where one of the old Common gates once stood, and Blackshore. Sometimes, so-called higher authorities refer to it as Harbour Road, sometimes they regard it as nothing more than an extension of York Road but locals know it as Carnsey or Caunsey Road, the name deriving from the fact that since time immemorial it has been a causeway, a raised path, crossing the marshland.

Water Towers, Carnsey Road, 1960s

CAUTLEY ROAD

A Reverend William G Cautley is listed as a subscriber to Wake's 1839 tome but he lived in Earsham, not Southwold. No, it is another holy Cautley, the Reverend Probin Littler Cautley, commemorated here. This Reverend Cautley was the incumbent of St Edmund's from 1877 to 1891 and one of his claims to fame was that he was one of the seven people who in 1884 proposed that a Golf and Quoit Club be formed in Southwold. This was pretty revolutionary for the time as there were then only three other golf clubs in East Anglia. P.L. was also a councillor though, and it is more likely that it was that association that led to his memorialisation. He is recorded as living, with his housekeeper, at 24 South Green.

Pin Cottage at 22 South Green was once the site of the Nord Sea Inn, the alehouse of choice of the fishermen of Primrose Alley. When it was closed the fishermen transferred their allegiance to the Red Lion, wearing a path across South Green as they did so. The Council, exhibiting an astounding lack of common sense and understanding of human nature, tried to stop them doing this. The inevitable failure of this enterprise and the concomitant ridicule was forestalled by the Reverend Cautley who came up with the pragmatic suggestion that a permanent path be made across the green instead. It would be agreeable to think that it was in recognition of this service in saving the Council's face that it decided in 1903 to immortalise him.

CENTRE CLIFF

Centre Cliff is the stretch of Marine Villas between South Green and the seaward end of East Street built to accommodate the first wave of well-heeled visitors (see Chester Road). Prior to that it was known as Long Island Cliff after the beach beneath it.

When fishermen plied their trade from the beach and indeed lived there or on the scores leading down to it, they divided it into sections each of which bore a name with an American connection. The South Cliff was New York, the Centre Cliff, Long Island as mentioned, then there was California to the south, parallel to Ferry Road and, further north, the Klondyke after which the play area opposite the Pier is named. Robert Wake is most fulsome about the Centre Cliff houses: 'they present a very handsome and commanding appearance not less on account of the gracefulness of the buildings themselves, than of the loveliness with which their enclosed shrubberies and tastefully arranged and very carefully tended flower pots, have contributed to their decoration'. He would say that wouldn't he, after all he lived in one of them.

Fulsome though Robert Wake was, these villas are an attractive group and would have been even more remarkable when the four-storey Centre Cliff Hotel was still there; unfortunately, its upper two floors had to be removed after the Second World War, the troops billeted there having behaved less than respectfully towards the fabric of the building.

Centre Cliff, early 1900s

CHESTER ROAD

Chester Road is tricky. Southwold does not name streets after places and apart from Victoria and the Marquis of Lorne royalty does not get much of a look in either so it's highly unlikely to be named in honour of an Earl of Chester, one of the many titles the heir apparent is traditionally burdened with. There was a G J Chester who wrote Antiquities of the Valleys of the Waveney and Yare in 1855 but this records findings in Dunwich, Hoxne and Wangford, hardly a recommendation to the burgesses of Southwold.

Chester Road was part of the late Victorian building surge. An 1891 map marks it, along with Dunwich Road and Stradbroke Road, as prospective, and it first appears in the municipal rolls in 1895. However, as late as 1910 photographs show that although there was a General Stores on the north side of the junction with Stradbroke Road - later George Bumstead's wonderful grocer's shop and now residential - there was nothing between the roadway and the lighthouse; the terrace of houses on the south side of the road appeared later.

So, if the road was not named after royalty or a city the other side of the country, why Chester? Well, there was a Colonel Heneage Charles Bagot Chester, of the 27th (Inniskilling) Regiment of Foot who fought in the Indian Mutiny on the north-west frontier. Born on February 12th 1836, he is recorded as having first married Madeline Elizabeth Massey with whom he had two sons, Captain Greville John Massey Bagot-Chester who died in 1917, and Hugh Augustus Bagot-Chester who lived until 1938. The Colonel himself later married a rich widow. Her previous husband was Thomas Bowen Sheriffe whose family owned Henstead Hall and Centre

Cliff then regarded as one of the grandest, if not the grandest, house in Southwold. Centre Cliff had been built by the Sheriffe family as part of a speculative investment to house upper class families who wanted to spend their summers by the sea. Holiday homes not a new phenomenon then.

Anyway, lucky Heneage came by these two prestigious homes courtesy of his rich widow. He is buried in Ashstead in Surrey but there is a memorial plaque dedicated to him in Henstead Church. None of which suggests any particular reason for Southwold to immortalise him. He was, however, one of Suffolk's Justices of the Peace and, maybe more to the point, one of the original directors of the Southwold Railway. Perhaps that was why.

CHILD'S YARD

The 17th century map shows a footpath following the course of the present Child's Yard from the Market Place but going right through to Mill Lane. It was unnamed, of course, like all other roads at the time and anyway Edmund Child had yet to arrive in town.

He was born in Great Yarmouth in 1781, became an iron founder and, for some reason best known to himself, re-located to Southwold in the early 1800s. He lived at 6 Market Place, now Denny's, and established his foundry at the rear of his house. In 1841 his son, George Edmund Child, inherited the property and the business. He had also inherited his father's skills being a brilliant, innovative gas engineer, responsible, in time, for the design of the traditional gas holders which were once such a feature of towns across the country. He made the equipment for the Southwold Gas Company which stood where Crick Court now is in Station Road, and also the gas holder in Blyth Road built in 1935 (the site of which British Gas shamefully refused to return to the Town Council). Child's foundry itself was the source of many items which still enhance the town: the church gates, the trough outside The Swan and, of course, the pump in the Market Place which still bears the legend "G E Child fecit".

Child's Yard

CHURCH GREEN

Informally known as Brewery Green and, according to Mrs Ida Critten writing in *The Story of Southwold* in 1948, also called Sawyer's Green after a carpenter appropriately called Sawyer, who once lived and worked there, Church Green is perhaps the least prepossessing of Southwold's greens. With the toilet block, the disregarded cycle rack plonked there by Suffolk County Council against the Town Council's wishes and, for many years, the refuse bins stored there by Waveney District Council, it has not been a pretty sight. However, the removal of the bins to the Pier car park and the recent landscaping undertaken by Waveney have improved the green's appearance and made it a slightly more inviting place.

Back in the 19th century though it was much more pleasant being a broad expanse accommodating the Town Hall and, as old maps show, providing the main access to St Edmund's. It was not until the late 1800s or early 1900s that the current main entrance to St Edmund's was formed. The 1839 map in Wake shows a solid wall between the church and Bartholomew Green and this was still the case in 1884. However, by 1904 the roadway on Bartholomew Green is shown on maps and, presumably, the use of the Church Green access declined. Its former monopoly of access is still recorded not only in its own name but in one of the local names for the alley leading from the green to Victoria Street: Parson's Cut. (Parson's Cut's other name, which does not recall the connection unless one of the church incumbents was heavy on the scales, is Squeeze-Gut Alley.)

CHURCH STREET

You expect a Church Street to lead directly to a church and Southwold's Church Street does not appear to do this. Bank Alley would seem a more reasonable candidate for the name and, as I noted under that heading, there are references to its being called Church Passage and Church Path. There is at least one well-respected local person who has argued both in public and in private that Church Street is named after one of its late 18th early 19th century residents, John Church, a master mariner, but his residence there post-dates the earliest references to the road's ecclesiastical connections. A Copy Ordinance from 1584 refers to the route as 'the little lane next to John Dates' and goes on to order the closing of the lane to carts and carters because of problems caused by their use of the lane. It states that "that Lane was laide out but for a bier waye and being but narrowe, divers tymes there hathe been little children put in jeopardy of their lives. And it is further considered that if carts sholde have passage that waie it sholde be so noyuse that if any corse sholde come that waie to church the bearers sholde goe over their shoes in the myer". As I set out earlier, Church Green originally provided the main access to St Edmund's. Further, a former site of the Parsonage was on the High Street where Buckenham House now is and Church Street leads directly from there to the church via Parson's Cut.

The row of cottages on the west side of the street are some-times romantically but erroneously said to have been built by Dutch prisoners of war. In fact they were built by the Free British Fishery a company which was established in 1750 by Parliament and which chose Southwold as its base. Half way down on the opposite side of the road there was for many years a builder's yard which was removed in 1876 and replaced by the Brickmakers Arms public house at 38 Church Street. This continued trading until 1958 but was subsequently demolished when the area was redeveloped by the brewery which skilfully hid its tun room behind a façade of house frontages.

The 1584 Ordinance stated that the road was narrow, and 'twas ever thus, although surprisingly, it is wider now than it was. On April 3rd 1930 the General Stores at the junction of the

High Street and Church Street was burnt down and this allowed that end of the street to be widened, not by much though, as the problems experienced by delivery vehicles and the oft times assaulted fabric of the chemist's shop testify.

Church Street, 1898

CONSTITUTION HILL

Why Constitution Hill? Why indeed. Don't ask me. The British don't 'do' constitutions after all and it seems unlikely that the Corporation was exhibiting a wry sense of humour and suggesting that walking up the hill might be good for one's health. There is, of course, a Constitution Hill in London and my best guess is that the hill was peopled by early second home owners who liked to remind the locals that in their other lives their next door neighbours were the Royal Family.

In the early municipal rolls the address of people living on the hill was simply given as South End but at the 1911 meeting councillors decided that "the hill from Messrs Debneys' corner to Ash Villa be named Constitution Hill". Messrs Debneys corner was where the Homestead now is; Ash Villa is still Ash Villa. The residents did not have to wait too long before they ceased to be South End. The re-naming was accomplished by 1913.

CUMBERLAND ROAD

Why would genteel Southwold name one of its streets after a man known as the Butcher of Culloden? The story recorded by Wake is that William Augustus, Duke of Cumberland, was returning from Scotland by sea after crushing the Jacobite Rebellion there. He had devised a new military strategy which he had deployed successfully at Culloden in 1748. It was not, however, his actions on the field of battle which led to his nickname but the subsequent slaughter of civilian highlanders, women and children. Not surprisingly this made him unpopular north of the border and according to Wake he was afraid that it might not have endeared him to people further south either. However, again according to Wake, when he landed in Southwold, presumably to re-provision or have a paddle, he was received like a hero and by way of thanks presented the town with the cannon sited on Gun Hill. This is all nonsense (see Gun Hill) but the Borough Council in the early 20th century presumably believed it and thought the name suitable for one of the roadways they were hard-surfacing. Interestingly the 1670-1725 map shows a property called Cumberland House on Gun Hill roughly where Gun Hill Place now is.

Prince William, Duke of Cumberland. Portrait by Joshua Reynolds, 1758

17th century and 18th century maps show a path following the course of the present Cumberland Road skirting the boundary between land marked as pasture and land marked as Corporation land and joining East Green to the footpath to the beach which later became Field Stile Road. The path was also the most direct route from the town to the lime kiln situated where Field Stile Road now meets Marlborough Road and later from the town to Bagot's Mill which stood, for its brief 35 year life, at the Cumberland Road/Field Stile Road junction and which ground flour for the local bakers until it was burned down in 1876.

Also, the stretch north of where St Edmund's Hall now is was formerly a rope walk a connection recalled in the name of one of the terraced properties on the seaward side of the road, The Old Rope House.

In 1891 the Borough Council had major road making schemes in mind and measured the lengths of various roadways in town preparatory to costing their upgrading. It lists the measurement of "Brewery to Glan-y-don" as 1518 yards. Glan-y-don was the former name of Dunburgh House on the corner of Field Stile Road and North Parade so perhaps the idea was to make a sort of ring road round the new North End development area. If that was the intention it was not carried through at the time because when Salisbury Road was extended in 1901 it is recorded that it was a cul-de-sac ending at St Edmund's Green.

The suggestion that the road be called Cumberland Road was first mooted at the meeting of the street naming meeting of the Council on 25th May 1911. It did not have to wait as long as some others it being formally resolved by the Council on 8th March 1912 "that the road from East Green to the bungalow on St Edmund's Green be called Cumberland Road".

DRAYMAN SQUARE

What an uneuphonious name that is and it does not slip off the tongue easily either. Sorry, anyone who lives there, but it is and it does not. We have the powers that were at Adnams to thank for it. The Town Council thought that the street names on the development on the former Adnams Distribution Centre site should reflect the land's association prior to its connection with the brewing industry and suggested Glebe Square because the land had once belonged to the church and is marked on old maps as glebe land. It is not even as if Drayman Square accurately reflects most people's perception of Adnams' use of that land.

Whilst I know that the lorries that cart beer about are called drays, what most people think of when drays are mentioned is the horse-drawn drays and whilst the horses did clop up and down to the Distribution Centre they were based in Mill Lane and that's the place people associate them with. Drayman . . . it suggests too that there was only one drayman and of course that's not true either. Draymen would have been worse, I accept, but in my opinion, Glebe Square would have been better and more appropriate.

DUNWICH ROAD

Anyone who knows anything about the history of Southwold would be surprised to find a street, even a shortish street, named in honour of its ancient and bitter rival, Dunwich. Further, it is not Southwold's practice to name its streets after its neighbours as I mentioned in the Introduction. No, Southwold, particularly in Victorian and Edwardian times, named its roads after people and I think that that was the case here.

The eldest son of the Earl of Stradbroke was called Lord Dunwich. The Earl of Stradbroke was a hugely important man in the area and naming a street after his son, especially one which branched off Stradbroke Road itself, would no doubt have gone down very well indeed. Documents from 1891 show Dunwich Road, together with Chester Road and Stradbroke Road, as 'prospective'. The Council was then developing what was called the North Cliff estates of which they formed part. Entries for Dunwich Road first appeared in the electoral roll in 1895.

EAST GREEN

No mystery here. East Green once comprised both East Green and the present St James Green and was the most easterly of the town's greens (see St James Green). It features as a space on the earliest map (1670-1725) and is marked as East Green on the 1801 Ablett map.

EAST STREET

No mystery here either. East Street runs eastwards from the middle of the town and is one of the town's oldest thoroughfares. The map purporting to represent Southwold between 1670-1725 shows roads following the lines of the present High Street, Queen Street and East Street but indicates that East Street stopped at the junction with Pinkneys Lane and the present Trinity Street, the land between there and the cliff edge appearing to be part of Pinkneys Farm. No Lord Nelson for heaven's sake.

EVERSLEY ROAD

In 2005 the Southwold Branch of the Royal British Legion wrote to the Town Council about the problems they had with post because the road where the Legion was, between Blackmill and Wymering Roads, did not have a name. They suggested Eversley Road because although Eversley School at the Wymering Road end of their road had ceased to function its buildings were still there and being converted. The Town Council agreed, took the matter up with Waveney District Council which is responsible for the naming and numbering of streets, and the hitherto anonymous strip of asphalt was christened. It was with considerable amusement therefore that I came across the 1911 Borough Minutes and discovered that Eversley Road had been proposed as the name for that roadway 94 years previously. Well, we got there in the end!

FERRY ROAD

The derivation is obvious because the existence of a ferry across the Blyth predates Dani Church by six centuries or so. The records of an Inquisition at Dunwich in 1236 state that Margery de Cressy, Lady of the Manor of Blythburgh and Walberswick, "was enjoined to keep a ferry boat at the side of the Blyth and exact customs - one halfpenny for man and horse" (which seems a lot of money for the time). The ferry crossing continued to be made by rowing boat for the next five and a half centuries. Inevitably during that time there were accidents, the most notable being in 1616 when 21 people returning from St James' Fair in Dunwich all crammed into one boat so overloading it that it capsized and all the passengers drowned. One of those on board was Elizabeth Yonges the daughter of the vicar of St Edmund's (see Youngs Yard).

In 1885 the River Blyth Ferry Company was registered and provided a chain ferry across the river which was worked by hand until 1899 when manpower was replaced by steam power. In this form the ferry functioned until 1941, its passengers in that time including the then Princess of Wales in 1906 and a troop of circus elephants transported carefully, one at a time.

Despite all that ferry-oriented history, Maggs in 1818 refers to the road as Jetty Road as does Wake in 1839. A note attached to an 1891 map records the length of the road from the Market Place to the ferry as being 5,418 feet but does not name it and in 1912 when the Council was setting aside money to make up various roads in town it agreed to hard-surface the road from "the Saltworks at the foot of Constitution Hill to the ferry" but, again, does not name the road despite the fact that it had proposed calling it Ferry Road at the street naming meeting the previous year. In 1923 the name Ferry Road finally appears in an official document.

FIELD STILE ROAD

As noted elsewhere, until the late 1800s, north of St Edmund's there was the area marked on the map in Wake's history as Corporation land (now Tibbys Green) and then open fields. The present Field Stile Road follows the boundary between the Corporation land and the open fields as far as the junction with the end of the Corporation land (the present Cumberland Road). It would have been natural for people going from North Green to the beach to walk along the boundary and the edge of the fields. The 1839 map also shows clearly the boundary turning awkwardly by the farm, where the hospital now is, as it does to this day.

Beyond the junction with the present Cumberland Road there was as early as 1839 a track which bifurcated roughly at the present junction with Marlborough Road, one branch marked as leading to the beach and the other going to the Brick Kilns. The building on the corner of Field Stile Road and Marlborough Road, Brick Kiln Cottage, recalls this connection. Presumably somewhere along this route there was at least one stile!

Some of the houses on Field Stile Road bear quite early dates, 1876 and 1881, but the road itself was not formed until 1895 when a contract was issued to build "a roadway over St Edmund's Green and a path on the north side thereof from the bungalow situate on the east side of the Green to the west entrance near the Roller Mills belonging to Hopkins, Smith & Girling". The Roller Mills or Flour Mills, later the Fordux Mattress factory, still stand, of course, at the North Green end of the road, now converted into flats and called St Edmund's Court. Strangely, the first reference to Field Stile Road in the municipal rolls appears to be 1902 when a Mr Crowdy is recorded as living there.

FOSTER CLOSE

Foster Close was named after the redoubtable Georgiana Fanny Julia Foster who when asked once what she thought of Southwold is reported to have said "Young man I am Southwold".

Fanny was born just outside Norwich in 1891 but moved to White Lodge overlooking the sea at the Gun Hill end of South

Fanny Foster, 1953

Green when she was only a few years old. Her father, Charles Foster Esquire, is recorded in White's Directory as living there in 1874 and, according to John 'Dusso' Winter, local fishermen always used to refer to White Lodge as Foster's House.

Fanny was educated at St Felix School and then escaped small-town claustrophobia by winning a place at Newnham College, Cambridge. Her fate, however, mirrored that of many intelligent daughters of the time: she had to return home to care for her ailing mother, and here she stayed until her mother's death in 1922 when a bequest from an uncle gave her her freedom. Her mind, however, even when her duty kept her in Southwold, was far from parochial; she had eclectic yet practical interests studying photography, book keeping and Serbo-Croat, as well as championing conservation and being one of the earliest to fight to save Southwold from developers and others who saw it solely as a money-spinner for themselves. To that end she was a councillor for 32 years, Mayor three times, an alderman and the last person to be elected a Freeman of the

Borough. Her citation recorded that she had been awarded the honour for her "untiring services to Southwold and vigilance in seeking to preserve all that is good in the life and character of the Borough". She would undoubtedly have had cutting but cogent things to say about Southwold's London-oriented businesses and those who present themselves as serving the town's best interests by promoting them.

Foster Close was built by the Borough Council in the mid 1950s when Fanny was an alderman and it first appears in the electoral roll in 1956. In 1973 Fanny was found lying unconscious in Gardner Road. She said later that she had been knocked down by a newspaper delivery boy cycling out of Strickland Place but she always refused to name him because she said that it had been her fault. She died the following year aged 83 and is buried in the churchyard.

FOX YARD

Fox Yard, the cul-de-sac off Gardner Road adjacent to the Red Cross Centre, was formerly Taylor's builder's yard and before that the site of Fulcher's smithy. It was sold in the 1990s to the A B D Fox Settlement Trust (more snappily known as the Fox Trust) which was set up in 1962 by Anthony Basil Darwin Fox, known as Tony, with the aim of providing a home or homes for elderly people in need who had been permanent residents of Southwold or its vicinity.

Tony Fox, born in 1902, was the youngest of six children whose father, Reverend William Fox, was a schoolmaster who moved to Southwold in 1913 because of ill health. His youngest children moved here with him, Tony's older sister, Nancy, attending St Felix School. Through marriage the Fox family was related to Charles Darwin and, furthermore, William Fox had been a friend of Darwin at Cambridge. He made it clear where he stood on the evolution argument by bestowing the name Darwin on both Tony and Nancy, a name the Fox Trust subsequently gave to the flats near North Green, Darwin Court.

Tony had trained as an analytical chemist and had worked in India but he too suffered ill-health and was invalided home. After Nancy had nursed him back to health he joined the Stock Exchange where he was clearly a canny investor, in time setting up a holding company and amassing a considerable fortune. Although based in London he shared Beacon Cottage on St James Green with sister Nancy and was well known in Southwold, particularly as a dab hand at bridge. He bought Blyth House and converted it to accommodate not only himself but also Nancy, their widowed sister, Joan, and their many dogs, each having their own en suite bedroom and sitting room - the siblings, that is, not the dogs.

Beacon Cottage

Although Tony was well known, Nancy was the permanent fixture and long time residents recall her in town invariably trailing dachshunds in her wake. She had been a brilliant tennis player, in 1925 playing Suzanne Lenglen, one-time Wimbledon Champion. Nancy used to recall that she managed to win two games. Councillor Sue Doy, herself a good tennis player, remembers in her turn, playing against Nancy. Anecdotes about Nancy abound, one of my favourites being that she called round on a local couple on their Golden Wedding Anniversary bearing a tin of Lyle's Golden Syrup as a gift.

Tony established the Trust because neither he nor his sisters had children to whom to leave his wealth and because he felt that Southwold had been good to the family. He died in 1969 and although by the 1980s the charity's property portfolio did include Darwin Court as well as Blyth House, little happened with his bequest until after Nancy's death in 1989 when the Trust became fully operational. It now owns 25 homes including the five in Fox Yard.

GARDNER ROAD

It is Gardner Road and not, as often written, Gardiner or Gardener, because it is named after Thomas Gardner, 1690-1769, the town's earliest historian whose book *An Historical Account of Dunwich, Blithburgh and Southwold* was published in 1754, and who was the local Salt Officer. Salt Officers were excisemen, the tax officers of the day. Salt was a vital commodity at that time particularly in the fishing industry where it was essential for curing fish, and duty was payable on its sale, export and import. As Southwold had its own salt pans and exported salt as well as using it locally Thomas was probably a very busy boy. He lived at the present 21, Park Lane, which is a bit surprising given that even as late as 1801 the road had been called Slutterton Lane (see Park Lane). The stews was hardly the place for Honour and Virtue (see below) to be expected to walk. It was convenient for work, though, the Salt Office being just round the corner on South Green. Gardner married twice as Wake recalls and, having waxed lyrical as only Wake can about Gardner's "treasured dust", he goes on to record that he was buried in the churchyard between his wives who had both predeceased him:

The inscription on the three stones which mark the respective graves of himself and both his wives as they sleep peacefully on either side of him partake of the quaintness and sobriety of the historian's living style... The stone on the south side records:- "To the memory of Rachael the wife of Thomas Gardner, who died 9th March, 1729, aged 35 years, and of Rachael their daughter, who died April 18th 1729, aged 12 years.

Virtue crowned during life
Both the daughter and the wife"

The stone on the north side is thus inscribed: "Mary, the wife of Thomas Gardner, died 3rd May 1759, aged 67 years.

Honour did ever attend
Her just dealing to the end."

The middle stone . . . bears this characteristic, or rather, paronomastic, notice: "In memory of Thomas Gardner, Salt Officer, who died March 30th, 1769, aged 79 years.

Between Honour and Virtue here doth lie
The remains of old antiquity."

A play on words indeed. Who was responsible, I wonder,

for this seemingly tongue-in-cheek inscription? I am not sure that even at the age of 79 Gardner would have relished his interred self being referred to as "the remains of old antiquity".

Gardner was theoretically immortalised at the 1911 meeting the Minutes of which record that the track between the Salt Works and Daisy Villa would be named after him. The Salt Works were at the town end of Ferry Road. All that remains of them now is the low brick building used as a Town Council workshop. Daisy Villa was adjacent to Woodley's Yard. Immortality was a while coming, however. Gardner Road does not appear in the electoral rolls until after the Second World War.

Thomas Gardner's house
in Park Lane

GODYLL ROAD

Poor William Godell: the town's greatest benefactor and he had to wait 456 years to have a road named after him. Even then his name was (possibly) wrongly spelt and he has since had to suffer all-comers who may never have read his will bandying his name about to justify whatever case they are trying to argue.

William Godell was one of the two bailiffs appointed under Southwold's first Charter in 1489. He calls himself a merchant in his Will but his business interests were wide. In 1485 and 1487 he is recorded as supervising people engaged in 'wafting' - provisioning the ships stationed by the king along the Norfolk and Suffolk coast to protect the fishing fleet - and in 1505, both Henry Godell and William Godell were included in a list of Staplers of Calais, the Staple of Calais being the main wool market in Europe.

Wool and fish were where the money was in the 15th century and William had the land and the ships to do very nicely thank you in both areas. His Will refers to his ships in Iceland, to fish, fishing nets and salt, as well as to his land "called Skylmans", land elsewhere, wool, sheep, cattle, horses and corn.

He was not short of a groat in this life then but like most of his contemporaries he was a deeply religious man who feared for his soul. He wanted to appear before his Maker in the best possible light and therefore although there are family bequests in his Will it is to the bailiffs and commonalty of Southwold that he left the bulk of his estate in 1509. Southwold has benefited ever since as the land he left comprised not only The Common and the marshes but probably all the land within the parish boundary apart from the area around the High Street and the church. It is surprising, therefore, that the ungrateful bailiffs and commonalty did not even consider commemorating their benefactor until 1911 and that then, having resolved that "the road from the south Common gate to the north Common gate" be called Godyll Road, did not in fact get around to actually doing this until 1965.

The map purporting to represent Southwold between 1670 and 1725 indicates, as mentioned previously, that there was a farm called Common Farm on the corner where St Barnabas now is. A footpath is shown following the boundary of this farm from the present York Road to the present Gardner Road along the exact route now taken by Godyll Road. Wake's 1839 map shows the same farm with indications of a partial track at the

Gardner Road end but by 1891 a map is marking the future Godyll Road as "To the Saltworks". However, a note attached to that map and dated April 3rd 1891 refers to a road following the line of the present Godyll Road, as Soane's Road.

Council documents from 1893 record that Mrs Charlotte Soans sold to the Council land bordering The Common which comprises the present York, Black Mill, Wymering and Manor Park Roads - possibly land which had originally belonged to the Common Farm. Mrs Soans had inherited this land in 1874 from a Mary Vernon Brame Leman, according to Maggs, and at the time of the sale she retained two small parcels of land either side of the entrance to Black Mill Road, the sites now of Forest Cottage and 33 High Street. By 1911 when the Council was applying its collective mind to street names Mrs Soans had died and no doubt the Council felt that any obligation to commemorate her had died with her, particularly as they had had to pay for her land whereas Godell's bequest had been charitable, albeit motivated also by a desire to ensure his soul a comfortable ever-after. Even so, action was less than swift. The Paving, Lighting and Public Health Committee directed its Surveyor on 13th December 1913 to "make up the road on The Common from St Barnabas to the gate at the end of Mill Lane".

No name then, and, as I intimated, no name for years. The houses built along the edge of The Common were simply addressed "Such and Such Villa", The Common, until 1965 when finally the name was bestowed. A long wait indeed for such a benevolent man. Why did they opt for the spelling they did? Difficult to be sure. Mediaeval spelling was erratic and even some of Godell's relatives spelt the name differently ie Godle but not Godyll. Perhaps in 1911 the Council opted for a phonetic version of the usual pronunciation. Who knows. At least now he is recognised.

GUN HILL

Gun Hill, pictured in 1829

The myth about Gun Hill and the Duke of Cumberland is referred to under Cumberland Road. The truth was set out clearly by Major-General P J Macksey in his booklet *The Southwold Guns.*

Southwold was originally supplied with guns during the reign of Charles I, between 1625 and 1639, long before the Duke of Cumberland was even a twinkle in his father's eye. The guns were sought to help protect ships anchored off the town from French privateers. In 1745, 120 years later, the town petitioned George II for new guns because the old ones had become dangerous to fire. This petition was granted in November 1745 and the town supplied with the six 18 pounders with carriages still mounted on the hill, and minor stores and ammunition. This was five months before the Battle of Culloden.

The rose and crown emblem on the cannon was used on ordnance from as early as the reign of Henry VII (1485-1509) until 1711. The guns were not new, then, when they were given to Southwold. In fact, as Major-General Macksey notes, they could, from the evidence of the rose and crown emblem alone, have dated from anytime within 226 years. However, he goes on to suggest, from their appearance, markings and dimensions, that they were made during the reign of Elizabeth I ie between 1558 and 1603. Major-General Macksey goes on to dismiss the Duke of Cumberland story by pointing out that the 18 pounder guns were typical battering pieces which would have needed heavy horses to drag them and that it was inconceivable that they were at the Battle of Culloden because neither the Highlanders nor the English had guns bigger than 4 pounders. He says further that there is evidence that Bonnie Prince Charlie never had more than two 18 pounders which were French guns sent to him with French reinforcements and not English ordnance marked with a rose and crown. Further, the Duke of Cumberland did not return from Scotland to London by sea and so could not have landed at Southwold. In fact he progressed triumphally back to London by land.

The origin of the story about the guns being presented to the town by the Duke of Cumberland appears to emanate from Thomas Gardner who wrote in his 1754 history that "on the cliff…are six eighteen pounders sent down by order of the Duke of Cumberland who landed there on the 17th day of October 1745". There is no mention there of Bonnie Prince Charlie or the Battle of Culloden, which as noted earlier took place the following year. It is possible, however, that the Duke did land at Southwold as Gardner records because after fighting the French in the Low Countries in 1745 he returned to London leaving Brussels on 14th October and reached his destination on 18th

October. There is no evidence, other than Gardner's statement, that the Duke did come to Southwold but as it was then, as now, a haven port, he may have taken refuge for some unknown reason and the great and the good of Southwold may have taken the opportunity to ask him to support their petition. We shall never know but at least we can rest assured that those guns have never been anywhere near Culloden.

Since then the guns have had a chequered history. Wake records that by 1803 they were lying abandoned in the grass; that in 1822 they were fired as George IV sailed by en route for Scotland and that this act of loyal support displeased him because all guns should have been dismounted; that despite this knock-back Southwold persisted in honouring royalty and fired a salute in August 1842 when Queen Victoria sailed by. Whether or not she was amused is not recorded but there was no amusement three months later when on 9th November the guns were fired to mark the birthday of the Prince of Wales. When one of the guns was being reloaded the charge exploded in the bore killing James Martin. The guns were never fired properly again and the ghost of James Martin is said to haunt the area to this day. I say "properly" because, of course, the Town Council has developed a tradition of 'firing' the cannons using theatrical flashes on significant occasions - Millennium Eve, the late Queen Mother's 100th birthday and, most recently, on 30th April 2011 to mark the wedding the previous day of Prince William and Catherine Middleton.

In the second world war the guns were dismounted and hidden. After the war they were relocated easily enough but their carriages had disappeared. They were not remounted until new carriages were made in 1956. Since 1972 they have been the responsibility of Waveney District Council.

Gardner, in his history, referred to the present Gun Hill as Eye Cliff, a name possibly derived from its being a good place for a look-out. Wake in 1839 calls the far end of the hill where Stone Cottage is, St Edmund's Hill although Maggs records that "in 1807 Capt Tindling R.N., John Benjafield Esq, Bury St Edmund's, and a Mr Spurling 1st built Houses upon Gun Hill - Rd Boyce, Builder".

So, a bit of confusion which, I suppose, persists because some of the houses which you might think are on Gun Hill in fact have a South Green postal address. That apart, Gun Hill's main problems now are people who think it is a grand place to park and rabbits which relish destroying the gardens of properties there, digging scrapes for the unwary to trip in and determinedly undermining the cliff. They'll be sorry when a cannon lands in their warren.

HIGH STREET

A street party in the High Street, 1887

There is no great mystery about High Street. It does not mean the street at the top of the hill nor the smelly street. It just means the main street. The word is derived from Old English heah which meant chief, principal, of great consequence. The chief town or capital in Anglo-Saxon was the heahburg whilst heahsetl was the high seat or throne. By the Middle Ages the word had taken on an additional meaning: in Chaucer you find heigh, hey and hy meaning the opposite of low and heighe and hye meaning high, on high, lordly and proudly. High as the opposite of low came to be the predominant meaning.

High meaning smelly did not appear to come into use until the 1800s when game started to be referred to as high. The

44

word's original meaning remains now only in expressions like high and mighty, Lord High Admiral, highwayman and High Street.

The High Street and East Street are undoubtedly the oldest streets in town, having developed from the spaces between the huddle of wooden buildings which housed the mediaeval population.

HOTSON ROAD

Hotson Road has a lot to answer for as it was driving along there when the first "I wonder" moment took place followed almost immediately by "And why Cautley?" and I was off, although, to be frank, there is such a confusion of Hotsons all over the historical records from the late 18th century onwards that I almost gave up as soon as I had started. Sorting out  one from the other is not helped by the practice of bestowing mum or dad's name on the firstborn, nor by the small pool of Christian names people chose from. Oh for a few Kylies and Jermaines to ease the detective process. In their absence here is my best guess.

Once upon a time there was a man called William Hotson. He was born in 1749 and married a young lady called Mary Bardwell, born in 1753, the daughter of Thomas Bardwell of

Uggeshall. William died in 1824, aged 75; Mary pre-deceased him, dying relatively young at the age of 52 in 1805, both deaths being commemorated on their now significantly eroded monument in St Edmund's churchyard. But the road is not named after them.

William and Mary appear to have had five children. The Reydon Parish Registers record the baptisms in 1783 and 1787 of Elizabeth, daughter of William and Mary Hotson, and William, son of ditto, respectively. The Southwold Records note Samuel, son of William and Mary Hotson being baptised in 1790. Burial Records show a Richard Hotson dying in 1862 at the age of 82. That would indicate his having been born in 1780 and hence potentially an older brother of Elizabeth and William. The Burial Records also refer to an Ann Hotson who died at the age of 41 in 1822, which could make her the second born, in 1781.

Richard Hotson is recorded as being a mariner. His wife was called Charlotte and they had a daughter named Emily, baptised in 1828. The 1844 White's Directory records that Charlotte was a milliner with premises in Queen Street. Richard's name appears in the Residential Rolls in the 1830s but he seems to have lived an un-noteworthy life apart from living to the ripe old age of 82 and fathering Emily when he was 48. (Emily herself inherited the longevity gene, dying in London in 1934 aged 86.) There is, though, a reference in the 1824 Gaol Book that reads "Robert Rogers, Mariner, put into prison for rioting with Mr Hotson". Richard would have been 37 at that time, past the first flush of youth but not too old for a brew-fuelled brawl with a fellow mariner, perhaps. . . . But the road was not named after him either.

What about William, the second son? Was it him? I don't think so. Maggs noted that on March 28th 1849 "Mr William

Hotson of this parish went under an Operation for the Stone." Anyone familiar with Pepys's account of an operation for the removal of a 'stone' will currently be wincing. Strong though a man must be to survive such a procedure - and he did, living a further three years until 1852 - I doubt if anyone in the 18th century would have considered it worthy of memorialisation.

Then there was Sam, the youngest son. He is recorded in the Southwold Registers of having married Mary Briggs of Dunwich on 4th April 1815 when he would have been 25. They had a daughter, Jane, in March 1816, Sam being referred to as a mariner. I could find no record of Sam's death locally but Maggs notes that on December 3rd 1851 he sold the effects of Mr Sam Hotson who had left to reside in London; that might explain it. There is also in Maggs an earlier reference to Mary Hotson buying the house of the verger, George Naunton, for £93 in 1839. Had Sam and Mary set up separate establishments by then or was this another Mary Hotson? There are further references to a Mary Hotson who ran a school. White's Suffolk of 1844 mentions a Mary Hotson under its heading Academies and the 1864 Harrod's Directory of Suffolk records Miss Hotson's Ladies Seminary. Sam's Mary would have been 52 in 1844 and daughter Jane 48 in 1864, old enough to have taken over the school from Mum. As for Sam, there was clearly no love lost. Mary and Jane are both buried in St Edmund's churchyard but there are no affectionate references to Sam on their gravestone. If his family did not choose to remember him I am sure the town would not.

So, we move on to the next generation. There was another William Hotson, perhaps the son of the William who endured the operation for the stone, whose wife was called Ann. She died on March 15th 1875 aged 61. Her memorial in St Edmund's churchyard refers to her as the "beloved wife of William Hotson (late of Islington)". The memorial also testifies that William died on November 8th 1889 aged 75. I thought the reference to Islington tied in with the reference in the subscribers list to Wake's 1839 history of a W C Hotson described as a resident of Lincoln's Inn Fields but William, husband of Ann, would have only been a whippersnapper of 25 in 1839 and not really a candidate for subscribing to a history of Southwold so there must have been another branch of the family in London; perhaps the William who married Ann was the son of W C Hotson who was, maybe, the son of a brother of the William who married Mary Bardwell. Anyone still with me? And perhaps when Sam left Mary and Jane and Southwold in 1851 he went to live with his rich London relatives. Perhaps, perhaps.

Returning to facts. . . . This last William Hotson who would have been born in 1814 and who married Ann is recorded by Maggs of having paid a Mrs Souper £700 for a property on South Green in September 1865. He subsequently knocked Mrs Souper's house down and rebuilt it as Acton Villa in 1872. This William Hotson was a tailor who went on to serve as a councillor from 1879 until at least 1885 and featured in the infamous lampoon written by the then Town Clerk, Harry Read Allen, about the candidates for the November 1880 elections:-

Hotson, W (Retired Tailor)
> To be the worst smacks somewhat of renown
> So hail! Thou least loved man of all the town.

Not popular then so why was a road named after him? Well, as well as being a tailor William Hotson owned land. When the then Council decided to extend the town northwards although it owned a lot of the land between the church and Buss Creek - the Town Farm - there were two other landowners there also. One was George S Alefounder whose land lay alongside the present Marlborough Road and the other was William Hotson. A map accompanying an indenture of 1888 shows William Hotson's land in the middle of the tract between Alefounder's land and Station Road covering almost exactly the present Hotson Road between Marlborough Road and St Edmund's Road and the houses and gardens either side of it. So Hotson Road it was. Mr Alefounder did not get a road named after him but then Mr Alefounder was not a councillor.

LORNE ROAD

I have often wondered why so many pubs are called the Marquis of Lorne. Southwold had one - on the corner of Field Stile Road and the High Street - and it has Lorne Road as well.

The Dictionary of National Biography records a Lord of Lorne in the 14th century. Subsequently Marquess (Marquis) of Lorne was, and perhaps still is, a title given to the eldest son of the Chieftain of the Duke of Argyll. The Marquis of Lorne so often immortalized by alcohol outlets, however, was one John George Edward Henry Douglas Sutherland Campbell, Marquess of Lorne and ninth Duke of Argyll, who, in 1871, married the fourth daughter of Queen Victoria, Princess Louise. The story goes that Queen Victoria wanted a British husband for Louise and checked out potential suitors by inviting them to Balmoral; not everyone's idea of a relaxing few days away with or without one's contraceptive equipment. Young John Campbell was one of these. He was described as being "short, stout, with yellow hair, regular features and a good complexion". Victoria apparently liked everything about him but his nasal voice, the result of a cricket ball in the face at Eton. He and Louise married on 21st March 1871.

Southwold Council, ever loyal, had agreed six weeks earlier, on 3rd February, to back a proposal of Cllr Vertue that Meeting House Lane be renamed Lorne Road. In 1878 Victoria appointed her son-in-law Governor of Canada but Louise did not settle there and Victoria missed her so they returned and the Marquis spent much of his later years writing and managing his Scottish estate.

Prior to its renaming the road had been referred to sometimes as Philpot's Lane after Alderman Philpot who lived on the corner in what is now May Place. For most of the previous two hundred years, however, the name was, as mentioned above, Meeting House Lane because, as Wake records, a fish office there was registered on June 20th 1694 as the place of worship of the Southwold Dissenters: "Successive generations of the Southwold Dissenters continued to meet in this building for a long period till its dilapidated state led some individuals of the congregation to commence a subscription towards raising a

Card commemorating the engagement of John Campbell, Marquess of Lorne and Princess Louise, 1870

fund for erecting a new meeting house. In order to obtain an eligible spot for their purpose they laid out £450 in purchasing premises in the High Street, formerly used as the Custom-house." Maggs records that the Old Meeting House was sold by auction on 1st June 1837 to Samuel Wayth for £124 and that the following July it was pulled down and a house built. Meeting House Lane having lost its Meeting House the only surprising thing about the change in name is that it took so long and that the years between the Dissenters' move and the marriage of Princess Louise did not throw up another historical personage more worthy of recognition than the Marquis of Lorne, yellow hair and a good complexion notwithstanding.

Eva and Anne Walker in Lorne Road, early 1900s

MANOR FARM CLOSE

Manor Farm was one of the small farms between the High Street and The Common. The 17th century map shows a road where Manor Farm Close now joins the High Street albeit not curling round the back of the shops as it does now.

In the 17th century the Manor House was further along the High Street, roughly where Buckenham House now is, and its grounds extended to Mill Lane. The present Manor House in the High Street is a later building, its name reflecting the site of the former farm rather than the original Manor House. The early map indicates that Manor Farm had a moat and trees near its boundary with The Common where the gardens of Church House and Homeleigh now are.

MANOR PARK ROAD

Manor Park Road was part of the Council's West End Estate development. The Council had acquired the land from Mrs Charlotte Soans (see Godyll Road). Given the streets which were developed - York Road, Godyll Road, Black Mill Road and Wymering Road as well as Manor Park Road and the land which Mrs Soans retained - this land would seem to comprise Barnaby Farm and Common Farm as they appeared in the 17th century map, land which on the early 19th century Ablett map appears to be jointly owned by a Mr Dawson and a Mr Cann and which, as mentioned under Godyll Road, Mrs Soans inherited in 1874. Why Manor Park Road? The road follows the route of the old track between the site of the old, small farms and The Common which led to Manor Farm but no doubt common sense recognised that having a Manor Farm Road and a Manor Farm

Close was a recipe for postal disaster. Perhaps the powers that be thought that including the word 'Park' gave the name an up-market ring. Whatever the case it appears in the 1903 electoral roll as Manor Park Road.

However, in 1911 the Council, perhaps also puzzled by the grandiose 'Park', proposed a simpler name, Manor Road, a proposition vigorously opposed not only by Mrs Soans but also by a Mr A Fairweather of Redthorne, Manor Park Road, who wrote in a letter to the Council dated November 27th 1911: "The present name has been in use for 12 or more years and during that period has become known to your fellow townsmen and the public generally; to mutilate or alter it would cause confusion and would be of absolutely no benefit or advantage to anyone." The Council backed down and it has been Manor Park Road ever since.

MARKET PLACE

I do get fed up with correcting people who insist on saying Market Square because it quite clearly isn't. In the recent past some might have said with justification that it was not much of a market either and the market area is, admittedly, small but most people do seem to agree that there has been a vast improvement in the number and variety of stalls since the Town Council took back responsibility for the markets from Waveney District Council in March 2008.

Southwold had held a Thursday market since 1220 and its Charter granted by Henry VII in 1489 gave the town the right to hold a market on Monday as well although the precise site of those markets was not specified. As the late A F Bottomley records in *A Short History of Southwold* "the Market Place was dominated by the Market Hall, a leaden roofed building raised above the sheltering stalls on eight pillars and probably octagonal in shape."

This was where the town's 'petty' business took place and it seems to have needed frequent repairs: it burnt down in 1659, of course, along with almost everything else in town but its 1666 replacement needed considerable work done on it nine years later and then again in 1714 when new timbers were bought for it. The Market Hall then survived almost another century until in 1809 it was judged to be "in a very ruinous and decayed state likely to endanger the lives of His Majesty's subjects passing and re-passing" and it was taken down. Maggs records too that "the old gaol and the shambles in the Market Place were taken down and rebuilt in 1819".

The East side of the Market Place early 1800s featuring the old jail, from an engraving by Hamlet Watling

The Market Place

The shop currently housing Collen & Clare, 25 Market Place, was there, however, when the Market Hall and the shambles were. It was built in the 16th century and remains one of the oldest buildings in Southwold to have survived the 1659 fire. The adjacent buildings, the butcher's and greengrocer's, are early 19th century but when originally built mirrored the older building. Number 21, Market Place, the greengrocer's, once housed the town gaol and there are local stories about a tunnel beneath the Market Place connecting the gaol to the Town Hall where the trial of minor misdemeanours took place. This may or may not be true but the cellars of the Town Hall do still contain late 18th century or early 19th century lock-ups which I imagine were used as holding cells when Petty Sessions took place upstairs in the present Council Chamber. In the early part of the 20th century the ground floor of the Town Hall housed the

55

town's fire engine which emerged through double doors where the ground floor windows now are. The pump which graces the Market Place was made in Child's Foundry as noted earlier and presented to the town in 1873. Although the Market Hall is long gone the Town Hall has been in the Market Place ever since and continues to be the hub of the town's activities throughout the year on civic occasions, Christmas Lights Switch-on Night and so on.

MARLBOROUGH ROAD

Routine local quiz question: what was Marlborough Road called before it was Marlborough Road? Yes, indeed: Corporation Road. Why it was called Corporation Road is easy. It was built across land owned by the Corporation. Even as Corporation Road, though, it was a relative newcomer. It was part of the major building boom in the late 19th century when land belonging to the Corporation, to William Hotson and to the Trustees of George S Alefounder was developed and Pier Avenue, Hotson Road, St Edmund's Road, Cautley Road, Field Stile Road and Corporation Road appeared. Corporation Road is marked as such on an 1891 map and figures in the municipal rolls in 1895 but by 1911 the natives were restless and the following petition was presented:-

> We the undersigned Ratepayers, Inhabitants and Tenants of premises in Corporation Road, Southwold, Memorialize the Southwold Borough Council to rename the Corporation Road, Marlborough Road, and we trust our request will be granted by the Council.

It was, but not until 1938.

The Marlborough Hotel was built on the corner of the then Corporation Road and Dunwich Road in 1900 and no doubt inspired the residents to press for the name change, but why Marlborough Hotel in the first place? Corporation Hotel clearly did not have a glamorous ring and perhaps a Dunwich Hotel in Southwold would have been a genuflection to the Stradbrokes too far - although I am told by Dusso Winter that locals did refer to the Marlborough as the Dunwich Hotel; typical bloody-mindedness that.

The hotel itself was damaged by enemy action on 15th May 1943, demolished and ultimately replaced by the complex of flats on the corner. Anyway, back to Marlborough. The Duke of Marlborough, despite suffering the vagaries of political life in the 17th and 18th centuries and ultimately falling out of favour with Queen Anne, had been, after all, one of Britain's great generals and, through the Spencer Churchills and the Blenheim connection, his name continued to have grand connotations. I have no idea, however, why it took the Council until 1938 to accede to the petitioners' request. Perhaps the Borough Council wanted people to remember that the land on which their homes were built had belonged to the town; perhaps they were piqued that residents were so keen to dismiss the connection; or perhaps, like many things in local government, the petition just slipped to the bottom of the pending tray.

MIGHT'S ROAD

A name little used, Might's Road. In most people's minds Might's Road tends to be subsumed into Station Road and, in a way, it was ever thus. Until the advent of the railway in 1879 the whole length of roadway from the end of the High Street to the bridge was marked on maps merely as to or from Wangford, or Reydon High Road. It's probably overlooked because no-one lives there. They did once, though. In 1815 a house was built roughly where the Fire Station is today. It was called the Gatehouse and erected beside it was a structure many people would like to see reintroduced: a gate across the road. It only lasted until 1837, however. There might, of course, be people living in Might's Road again when the development on the former garage site is completed. Might's Bridge, on the other hand, is another story. A F Bottomley notes in his *Short History* that the bridge was known by the name Might's Bridge as early as 1256 which suggests that it predates any other name in town.

So why Might's? I am no etymologist so what follows is conjecture but I think that there are two prime possibilities. 'Might' whilst always meaning power and strength used to be used also in a broader sense to mean the extent of someone's dominion or rule: the king's might, for instance, meant not only his power but also the area over which he exerted that power.

So, Might's Bridge could have marked the extent of the power of whoever controlled Southwold. Bottomley also records that in 1256 "the Sheriff of Suffolk was ordered to make a perambulation between the land of the Abbot (the Abbot of Bury, then lord of the manor of Southwold) and that of Hubert de Bavent in Easton" and it is in that context that Bottomley says that Might's Bridge was "known even then by that name".

Alternatively, or, perhaps, as well as, Might's could derive from the Old English 'metan' which means not only to meet but also to cross. The bridge was where Southwold and Reydon met and was also the crossing place over Buss Creek. The Old English noun associated with the verb 'metan' is 'mytting' and it seems reasonable to surmise that Mytting's Bridge might have been contracted over the centuries to Might's.

Left: approaching the old Might's Bridge, built in 1783

Below: Building work on Might's Bridge, 1926

MILL LANE

A sketch of the White Mill circa 1880

It is a well-worn route, Mill Lane. It appears on the 1670-1725 map leading, not surprisingly, to a windmill on The Common. That would have been the Town or White Mill which stood on the south-eastern side of The Common as early as 1658 - roughly where the bushes are between the golf course and the rugby pitch (when they haven't been cut down in order to get at the rabbit warrens that is). It was rented from the town, the rents recorded in 1723 as being £4.6s.8d per annum. Standing as it did on a rise in an exposed part of The Common it would have certainly caught the wind as anyone trying to kick a rugby ball there would confirm; too much in truth. In 1738 a lady called Rebecca Chilvers was killed by falling debris when the mill almost blew down in a gale. Forty years later after further episodes of structural damage it was pulled down.

Another mill built on the same site suffered a similar fate in 1795 at which time it seems finally to have registered with the powers that be that maybe a less exposed site might be a good idea (see Black Mill Road). The remains of the White Mill were finally removed in 1898. Despite the logic of calling the route to the mill Mill Lane the road has, in fact, had several other names in its history. Although the map in Wake's 1839 history has it marked as Mill Lane the 1801 Ablett map calls it Rosemary Lane and there is still a Rosemary Cottage in the lane. There are also occasional references to its being called Chapel Lane, which makes sense because as James Maggs records, a Mr William Samkin built a Wesleyan Chapel there in 1799. A F Bottomley, in his introduction to his edition of Maggs's Diary records that from 1806 to 1810 a Mr Tory used this Chapel as a very early school teaching children to write using a sand tray and to read and spell, and not just on Sundays but on weekdays as well; very progressive, but then that's Southwold. Mr Bottomley also notes elsewhere that between 1850 and 1868 the road is referred to as Gaol Street, no doubt because the gaol stood on the corner of the Market Place opposite.

Finally on an 1891 map and on the note attached to it the route is called Mill Road and Mill Lane Road respectively and its length quoted as 561 feet. Some consensus was eventually achieved, though, and Mill Lane it was throughout the 20th century and still is, although Swimming Pool Lane might be an option for the future.

A young Douglas Palmer, with Mill Lane behind, 1920s

NORTH GREEN

North Green is North Green for obvious directional reasons. It was where the town began until Station Road was developed in the late 19th century and is named as such on the 1801 Ablett map. Even on the putative 17th century map it appears, in its present shape, as open ground crossed by paths in the same position as the paths which cross it to this day. The map shows a building on the green itself roughly where the library is, a row of buildings where there is still a row of old cottages and a farm, Chapel Farm, where Darwin Court now stands.

NORTH PARADE AND NORTH PARADE GARDENS

Until the Victorian building surge the whole of the area north of St James Green was referred to as North Cliff. Land near the Pier comprising the present Pier Avenue and Hotson Road, had been sold to the Coastal Development Company (see Pier Avenue) but the land nearer the town centre remained in municipal hands and is referred to in Council documents as the North Cliff Estates whilst the present North Parade, as late as 1891, is called North Cliff Road. In May 1900, however, the Coastal Development Company was complaining to the Council about the latter's failure to make up North Parade so clearly the name change had been agreed sometime in the intervening nine years. North Parade Gardens would have been part of the land sold to the Coastal Development Company which certainly formed the putting green that separates North Parade Gardens from North Parade itself.

above: North Parade

below: North Road

NORTH ROAD

Roads with a compass point in their name tend to go in that direction which, of course, North Road does not; it runs east/west. It is, however, the most northerly road in town apart from the stretch of Might's Road between it and the bridge. There was a man called Edward North who was one of the town's bailiffs in the 1680s but he was an "appointed man" under the so-called usurping charter and so not likely to have endeared himself to Southwold. More to the point, the arable land surrounding the town in the Middle Ages was divided into three open fields and the Town or North Field on its northern side was the last to survive. It provided almost a tenth of the Corporation's income and, according to Bottomley, was invariably mortgaged to the hilt because of the town's parlous financial state. It is this North Field connection that the road name records. A 1904 map has North Road marked on it but shows no houses there. The houses on the northern side of the road, Might's Cottages and Town Farm Cottages, were built by the Corporation and opened on 8th June 1914.

PARK LANE

As most local pub quiz players know Park Lane was known in the 1700s and as late as 1801 (Ablett's map) as Slutterton Lane; always a source of amusement, that one of the town's grander streets should once have been a mean, grubby track named after its foremost traders. Records indicate that by 1816 there may have been some attempts at reform, the roadway being variously referred to as Fryers Lane or Black Friars Lane and also as Chapman's Lane. James Maggs lived at 20 Park Lane from 1858 until his death in 1890 and he records that on 25th August 1873 Mr Edward Chapman's house in Park Lane was struck by lightning. Perhaps the Chapmans had had a family home there in the 18th century or earlier. Certainly by 1839 it was Park Lane as Wake's map records. The map shows a large property at The Common end of the road called Park Villa, now subdivided, whose grounds extend a third the length of the road and back as far as Skilman's Hill as they still do. But why Park Lane? It does not lead to a park. No, it does not but, like Constitution Hill it has a London connection; anyway, Common Lane would have

had echoes of its earlier name and no doubt worthy Hanoverians were anxious that their fragrant wives and daughters should not be associated with anything so indelicate.

The former School of Industrial Art, Park Lane

PIER AVENUE

Pier Avenue, beloved by boy racers, being the widest, straightest street in town, was built by the East Coast Development Company (later the Coast Development Corporation) across the Town Farm lands it bought from the Southwold Corporation in 1897 for £8000. The Company was keen to cash in on the increasing popularity of the east coast resorts and did so by building a series of piers which the Belle Steamers could call at, and by providing other amenities for the passengers disgorged from said steamers. The Company sold its scheme to the Corporation by promising not only visitor attractions but houses too : planning gain not a new phenomenon then. As well as the Pier, completed in 1900, the Company had built the Grand Hotel by 1902 and also the tennis courts and bowling green where the skateboard park and putting green now are. Having provided these facilities the Company was keen to make sure that as many people as possible used them and so constructed Pier Avenue from the Pier to the station, also building the Station Hotel, later the Pier Avenue Hotel and now The Blyth, to accommodate visitors arriving by the Southwold Railway, and possibly The Cecil Hotel, now Lancaster Court, midway down the road.

The specification for making up Pier Avenue was considered by the Corporation in 1900 and the Company's plans included not only the road but also sewers and other services for the housing plots. Although the Company con-structed the visitor amenities in good time and had sold £6000's worth of building plots by 1900, progress with the actual building was slow. The 1904 Ordnance Survey map

View from the Church Tower about 1910 showing The Cecil, now
Lancaster Court, and Marram House in Pier Avenue.

The view today

68

marks the Grand and Station Hotels but only one other property in the road, possibly The Cecil, whilst the Municipal Rolls for 1905 indicate that even then there were only two occupied houses in the road. Photographs taken around 1910 still show only half-a-dozen large properties in Pier Avenue and it was not until 1913 that the number of permanent residents there went into double figures. By then, however, the Coast Development Corporation was long gone. It had clearly over-speculated and under-accumulated and by 1906 was being wound up.

Development was slow until the 1930s when a building firm called Palfreys took a hand. They built the run of semi-detached houses on the north side of the road, now numbers 22 to 52, and also the cul-de-sac of bungalows opposite. By 1946 there were 55 permanently occupied properties in Pier Avenue and 95 registered electors.

A fascination for children are the topsy-turvy houses, at the junction with Marlborough Road, 70 to 78 Pier Avenue. Built around the late 1960s these represent a feat of architectural ingenuity given that the brief was effectively to build houses in a pit. The Ablett map of 1801 indicates a pit in this area whilst the late 17th century map marks brick kilns here. This would make sense because as Dr D W Collings says in *"The Story of Southwold"* published in 1948 " to the north-west of the Grand Hotel a deposit of brick earth occurs which was used in recent times for making bricks (of red, sandy and soft nature). Near the land end of the pier a small area of clay - probably connected with that of the brickfield - is exposed by sea action at certain conditions of the tide". The land falls abruptly away from Pier Avenue at this point and it is more than likely that this was the result of excavations for the brick earth or clay. The solution to the problem of how five houses with prestigious Pier Avenue addresses could be built in a hole was to give them front doors at first floor level accessed by walkways, four off Pier Avenue and one off St Edmund's Road.

The rest of Pier Avenue was developed in a more piece-meal way: a mixture of detached and semi-detached houses, Council housing and bungalows. Its crowning glory is, of course, the telephone exchange. Often unnoticed, which is frankly the best way to deal with it, it is an unkempt, brutalist structure which with its chain-link fencing, communications mast and officious warning notices could be taken for a prison if the gate were not usually open. A particularly attractive touch is the water-stained curtain in the upstairs window. It is surprising given the premium on land in Southwold that BT did not sell it off years ago.

Three former Town Mayors still live in Pier Avenue which is a pretty surprising statistic when you first encounter it. However, it is here in the north end of town where permanent residents are still in the majority, manning the barricades against the insidious creep of second and holiday homes. How much longer they can hold out is anyone's guess. Pier Avenue is losing on average about two electors a year and whilst second and holiday homes do bring money into town they do not typically bring in people ready and able to turn out for Council meetings at least twice a month, come rain or shine, let alone take on the onerous duties of being Town Mayor.

PINKNEYS LANE

The first car driving against the one-way flow in Pinkneys Lane is, given the vagaries of our climate, a surer sign of summer than the first swallow. Pinkneys Lane is one of the town's oldest streets. It features on the 17th century map with an inn marked clearly on its junction with the present South Green where the Red Lion now stands. More to the point the map shows a Pinkneys Farm on the seaward side of the lane behind the inn where the walled garden now is. The 'farmland' encompasses all the land from the present South Green back to East Cliff - no houses and as noted earlier, no Lord Nelson. To compensate there was a chapel midway down the lane on the landward side. Ablett's 1801 map has the road marked Pinkenous Lane.

Pepys's Diary mentions a George Pinkney and there are numerous Pinkneys in Canada and the southern states of the U.S. Maidenhead has a large open green called Pinkneys Green which is apparently named after a Norman knight, Ghilo de Piquigny, who came over with William the Conqueror. Perhaps a relative of his moved to East Anglia and took up farming - but enough supposition.

Moving on to facts, there are several references in the 18th century Parish Registers to Pinkneys (or Pinkeneys or even in one instance Pinkenna) and at first sight these are confusing partly because, as mentioned under Hotson, people chose from such a small pool of Christian names, every other girl seeming to be called Mary, and partly because of the custom when a child died of bestowing the same name on the next child. The references to the Pinkneys do illustrate the tenuous hold on life which people had in the 18th century and the high rates of infant mortality. The first reference I could find was to Mary Pinkeney (sic) whose burial is recorded as being on 25th October 1727.

71

The next is to the marriage on 31st May 1736 of Simon Pinkney to Mary Crow. Following this are recorded the burials on 14th January 1738 of Elizabeth Pinkney (who is not recorded as a daughter and hence may have been Simon senior's mother or sister) and on 16th July of Simon, son of Simon and Mary Pinkney. 1743 saw the burial on 21st April of another Simon, son of Simon and Mary Pinkney and, the following year, on 29th June of Elizabeth, daughter of Simon and Mary Pinkney. That Elizabeth was only a few weeks old, the Baptismal Records for the Southwold Independent Chapel noting an Elizabeth Pinkney born in June 1744. Then the registers for 1746 record the burial of yet another Elizabeth, daughter of Simon and Mary Pinkney. In 1749 the Reydon Marriage Register records that on 31st December Simon Pinkney married Mary Witherell, a widow. He is not referred to as a widower but it seems likely that it was the same Simon and that his first wife Mary had died young worn down, perhaps, by childbirth and the grief of losing four children.

PRIMROSE ALLEY

This offshoot of South Green, now a desirable place to try to over-develop, was once far from the sweet smelling place its name suggests. Southwold, as noted previously, does not name its streets after things so a botanical association is unlikely. No, there were Primroses living here. A Benjamin Primrose appears in the 1811 census and there are references to a Sarah Jane Primrose living on South Green, at either 4 or 14, between 1894 and 1909. The present Primrose Alley was in fact once one of the roughest places in town. It was a fishermen's enclave, fishermen who after a hard stint at sea and probably nothing but herring for dinner, again, anaesthetised their sorrows at the adjacent Nord Sea Inn (see Cautley Road). No. 4 South Green is next to The Red Lion. Perhaps the path worn across South Green when the Nord Sea Inn was closed ended by Miss Primrose's house and that when the fishermen left their less than salubrious yard and an appealing name was required, Primrose was deemed an appropriate choice. Perhaps the Reverend Cautley was sweet on her.

QUEEN STREET AND QUEEN'S ROAD

It's a bit vague isn't it the non-specific Queen Street. For the worthies wrestling for a name it was perhaps an easy get out honouring as it could both the current Queen and any other Queen thereafter. Queen Street is the older of the two. It appears, albeit nameless, in the early 17th century map and features, this time named, in Thomas Ablett's 1801 map.

The Southwold & Reydon Corps of Drums in Queen Street, 1990s

Queen's Road did not appear until more than a century later. So, was it Queen Street in recognition of Queen Anne (1702-1714) whose Bounty benefited St Edmund's and thereby perhaps relieved the Corporation of some of the maintenance liabilities of the church which it had borne from time immemorial until 1819? Or was it in honour of the wife of one of the subsequent Georges?

It could have been more prosaic and, like much in Southwold, connected to alcohol. Bernard-Segrave Daly, in his chapter on Brewing and Pubs in *Southwold Portraits of an English Seaside Town*, records that The Red Lion Inn was purchased for £70 as the Queen's Head from Benjamin Harrington by Robert Thompson. The suggestion that the stretch of roadway "between the Red Lion and the Salt Works" be called Queen's Road was proposed at the 1911 Council meeting but this did not happen until sometime between 1920 and 1930.

ST EDMUND'S ROAD

What else could you call a road that appears, as you travel up it, to be heading straight for the church tower? What is surprising, though, given that the church is dedicated to St Edmund, that St Edmund is so significant to East Anglia and that the church itself has been in situ since the 1400s, is that the town waited until 1913 to name a road after him. The road was formed when the Southwold Corporation developed its Town Farm Estate. The farm itself, as noted previously, was roughly where the hospital is on Field Stile Road with some of its outbuildings being on the notorious bend leading to the top of the present St Edmund's Road. Southwold Corporation built Corporation

Cottages at the top end of the road in the early 1900s; a progressive move, this, as they were some of the earliest Council houses in the country. They were officially opened on 17th July 1905. Wake's Cottages further down the road, between the Hotson Road junction and Pier Avenue, are the town's only memorial

to its famous historian but at least he merited a row of cottages; Maggs got nothing.

ST JAMES GREEN

In 1227, seven years after Southwold gained the right to hold a market every Thursday it was granted the right to hold an annual fair on the Eve of Saints Philip and James Day, April 30th. This right was confirmed under the 1489 and subsequent Charters, the mediaeval fair later becoming the more variable Trinity Fair (now Charter Fair).

I was told by the late and much missed Ros McDermott, Town Mayor in 1991 and 1992 and the local history recorder for a decade or more, that in the Middle Ages Southwold was one of the authorised ports of departure for pilgrims going to the shrine of St James at Santiago de Compostela and that the scallop shells on the parapets of the houses along Centre Cliff were a later recognition of this, the scallop shell being a symbol of St James. She said she would dig out her background research on this but died before she could do so. My own research only revealed that the authorised ports were on the south coast and that the recognised pilgrimage routes, even from Walsingham, did not make a detour to Southwold.

However, I am indebted to Ros's daughter-in-law, Clare, for discovering that between 1235 and 1484 ships carrying pilgrims who were going to Santiago had to be licensed and that five of these licensed boats were registered to Southwold. Their owners were Richard Skilman (see Skilman's Hill) who had a boat called Mary licensed to carry 30 pilgrims, Robert Northfolk whose boat, Christopher, could carry 60, Henry Sow who had ships called James and Edmund, with no number of pilgrims specified, and Thomas Rogers whose boat Trinity similarly had no number of pilgrims specified. Henry Sow and Thomas Rogers had ships licensed elsewhere as well so they were probably not Southwold men but Richard Skilman certainly was and perhaps Robert Northfolk too although his surname suggests that he emanated from the other side of the Waveney.

It was not until a Council resolution of March 8th 1912 that St James Green achieved its own identity. Prior to that the whole of that area was called East Green. The name was probably chosen because the cottages on the northern side of the green were called St James Terrace and the present Stradbroke Road, St James Street, as Wake indicates in 1839.

SALISBURY ROAD

Salisbury Road first appeared in the 1890s as a cul-de-sac off Stradbroke Road and in November 1899 the Council agreed to build six houses there. Robert Gascoyne-Cecil, 3rd Marquess of Salisbury was Prime Minister at the time, as indeed he was for most of the period between 1885 and 1902. Prior to that he had worked under Disraeli as Foreign Secretary and been awarded the Order of the Garter  for leading the British delegation at the Congress of Berlin in 1878 which helped lead Britain to "peace with honour", allegedly, after the Russo-Turkish war. Queen Victoria thought he was a great patriot and that was no doubt good enough for Southwold.

The Council acquired a strip of land in 1901 intending to extend the road through to St Edmund's Green but in fact the road continued to be a dead-end until Cumberland Road was formed. The road was first surfaced in 1908-1909.

SIMON'S PATH

This name for the controversial cut through from Drayman Square to Tibby's Green memorializes Simon Loftus who was Managing Director of Adnams when the re-development of the brewery's Distribution Centre was being planned. Loftus Way was proposed originally. However there was already a Loftus Avenue in Reydon named after Simon's father, Pierse Loftus, who became a partner in Adnams brewery in the early 20th century and was instrumental in bringing much-needed capital and expertise to the business. The powers that be felt that confusion between Loftus Avenue and Loftus Way was inevitable, so Simon's Path it became.

SKILMAN'S HILL

There is possibly more historical fact attached to Skilman's Hill than to any other part of town. It is reputed to be the site of the castle which Richard de Clare, Earl of Gloucester, planned to

78

build to mark his lordship of the town after the Abbot of Bury St Edmund's, in 1259, exchanged the Abbey's manor of Southwold for a more manageable piece of land in Mildenhall owned by Richard. Unfortunately for Richard he did not have long enough left to build his dream castle, dying in 1262. His heir proved to have no enthusiasm for the project and all that remains is the mound on which the castle would have been built. Had more progress been made the hill might have been called Clare Hill or Gloucester Hill because Southwold continued to be held by the House of Clare for the next 200 years. However, they ruled as absentee landlords not venturing from their stronghold in Clare to listen to their tenants or kiss babies, just demanding their rents in herrings as well as money. If they had cared a little more and taken a little less they could have been immortalised. As it turned out the person paying the most herrings got that honour.

In 1391-2 the holding paying the most herrings and money was a tenement called Biskelees. A century later, in the 1490s, Biskelees was the property of Richard Gueman, also known as Skilman, and the land itself was also known as Skilman's manor. There are reputedly references to Richard Gueman and his wife in St Edmund's Church on the screen on the Lady Chapel and as noted above, under St James Green, Richard Skilman owned a boat licensed to carry pilgrims en route to Santiago de Compostela. Skilman's estate subsequently belonged to William Godell who bequeathed most of it to the town in his 1509 will, referring to it as "my land called Skylmans". The 17th century map shows the hill marked as Castle Mount. It appears as Skilman's Hill in the 1895 electoral roll.

SNOWDEN'S YARD

Snowden's Yard does not have its own identity in the electoral roll, being regarded as part of East Street, but it has its own sign so I am including it. There was a James Snowden Hurst who was Borough Surveyor and Sanitary Inspector from 1912 to 1940 but he lived at 10, Field Stile Road so I doubt, despite his long service to the town, that the yard was named after him. It is much more likely that it recalled the long residence there of Mr John Bullard Snowden. The municipal rolls record him as living at 14 East Street in 1895 and he is still there in 1915. The 1900 edition of Kelly's Directory describes him as an oil dealer. Members of the Snowden family continued to live in the yard until the mid 1930s when they moved to Reydon.

Snowden's Yard

SOUTH GREEN

South Green may be the town's biggest open space after The Common and the derivation of its name blindingly obvious, but it was christened a good 30 years after its siblings North and East Green. On the 1801 Ablett map the whole of the present Gun Hill, South Green and Constitution Hill area is marked as Gun Hill although by 1839 South Green, if not Constitution Hill, had acquired its own identity. South Green addresses appear in the 1895 municipal roll; at the same time addresses which subsequently became Constitution Hill are distinguished as being at South End. South Green is, of course, the venue for many of the town's long-standing events. Trinity Fair, now Charter Fair, has been held there since time immemorial.

In 1883 the then Corporation passed a resolution that the Fair should be held beyond South Green on the marshes near the Saltworks at the foot of Constitution Hill, a decision ignored by the showmen who set up on their usual pitches on South Green as their ancestors had done before them. In a fit of pique the Mayor, J E Grubbe, refused to open the Fair but that, of course, failed to stop the always wonderfully defiant townspeople from enjoying it as usual. Nothing daunted the Corporation had another go the following year, arranging for the showmen to be met by the might of Suffolk's Constabulary, each horse-drawn vehicle being allotted a policeman to lead it to the Corporation's preferred site at the foot of the Green. The Fair did stay there that year and the Mayor graciously opened it but the natives were restless and bitterly resentful; they demanded a poll and got one which unsurprisingly resulted in a majority for returning the Fair to its traditional site.

The Corporation retired to lick its wounds and all was quiet until 1912 when a Special Meeting, chaired by the Mayor,

E E Grubbe, son of J E Grubbe who had tried shifting the Fair before, decided that it should be moved to The Common. However, a few days later a petition signed by 273 burgesses was presented and eleven councillors asked the Mayor to reconsider the decision. Not having learned anything from his father's experience, he refused to do so and said that he would not officially open the Fair unless it was on The Common. This was too much for the townspeople and Herbert Adair Adnams, father of the present High Steward, John (J.A.) Adnams, seized not only the initiative but also the proclamation traditionally declaimed at the official opening of every Fair and read it out himself much to the jubilation of all right-thinking locals. This event was commemorated on its 80th anniversary in 1992 when John Adnams, then a town councillor, read the proclamation at the opening of the Fair instead of the Clerk.

South Green, early 1900s

On South Green the Fair has remained ever since. Given the strength of local opposition to its being moved one wonders why people continued to try to do so. It might be that in the late 19th and early 20th centuries many of the town's councillors were London based and possibly residents on a part time basis of up-market and desirable South Green. Perhaps they objected to their quiet enjoyment being disturbed on three days a year by the sight of other people having fun. More recently new residents of the town have been rumoured to have suggested in their turn that the Fair should be moved from South Green to The Common. As history has shown, Southwold fights for its traditions - not for nothing is the town's motto "'Defend they ryght" - and newcomers would do well to accept that the anomaly of having a funfair in so prestigious a part of town is one of Southwold's engaging quirks, and leave well alone!

SPINNERS LANE

The spinners recalled here were spinning not wool but hemp for the ropes required by the local fishermen. Ropes were made by walking with hanks of twine down what were called rope walks. As Zoe Randall explains in *Southwold: Portraits of an English Seaside Town* "the end of the hemp was attached to a large wooden wheel and the 'spinner', as he was called, walked backwards paying out the hempen fibres as he went. A boy was employed to turn the wheel, thus twisting the fibres into the initial strands". A Jasper Goodwin is recorded in 1841 as owning a twine ground near the Baptist Chapel. The Baptist Chapel, as Maggs recalls, "was built at the N.W. end of the Town upon Common Land granted by this Corporation for 99 yrs at 5s/- a year". The footpath edging The Common between the allotments and the back gardens of Station Road is, of course, still called the Rope Walk. Spinners Lane first appears in the municipal rolls in 1913

'Twizzle' at the end of Spinners Lane

STATION ROAD

Station Road is Station Road, not surprisingly, because it used to lead to the station - the terminus of the Southwold to Halesworth branch line. Prior to that, as mentioned under Might's Road, it was either unnamed on maps, marked with an arrow "to Wangford" or given the grand title "Reydon High Road" as it was on a plan of land leased to the Gas Light Company in 1840 (the Gas Light Company being based where Crick Court now is as mentioned under Child's Yard). There is, of course, still some confusion about its beginning and its end. You would expect it to start at York Road but it does not: because the town proper used to begin at North Green that's where the High Street began and ended too.

These days the High Street continues as far as Ferndale Cottage (beyond Field Stile Road on the opposite side) and that's where Station Road starts. It continues as far as Blyth Road where Might's Road begins. Work on the Southwold Railway began in May 1878 and the line was opened in September 1879. A map accompanying a conveyance dated 23rd February 1882 shows Station Road marked as such with the station in position. The station buildings and sidings were on the site now occupied by the Police and Fire Stations and the houses on the right hand side of Blyth Road. The station would have generated a lot of to-ing and fro-ing in and out of that part of the town and no doubt bearing the health and safety apparatchiks in mind the Corporation agreed in 1897 to form a concrete footpath from the station to Anchor Villa, in the High Street. (Anchor Villa is the building, formerly Ward's, but now Fat Face, its anchor still emblazoned on its façade despite subsequent reincarnations.)

STRADBROKE ROAD

Ah, Stradbroke Road. Here, indeed, might seem to be a prime example of corporate fawning. Well, yes and no. On Wake's 1839 map the road is a dead end of half-a-dozen houses finishing roughly where Chester Road now begins and called St James Street. By the turn of the century, however, like towns all over the country, Southwold was participating in the late

Victorian building boom. As mentioned previously an 1891 map in the archives marks Stradbroke, Dunwich and Chester Roads as "prospective" but they did not have to wait long. By 1895 Stradbroke Road is appearing in the municipal rolls. Ironically, at the time of writing it is conceivable that Stradbroke Road will soon disappear from the electoral rolls as it is now holiday-home country and has very few permanent residents.

I digress, however. Why Stradbroke? St James Street, after all, is a good name with historical relevance (see St James Green) but then Southwold's connections with the Earls of Stradbroke go back a long way too. In 1821 Sir John Rous of Henham (1750-1827) was made Viscount Dunwich and Earl of Stradbroke but forty years earlier, in the 1780s, he had been appointed a Commissioner of Southwold Harbour. Although he spent most of his time in London he appeared to have been a dutiful attendee of the meetings of the Commission which were held in The Swan. Whether this long distance commute was worth the effort is open to question. Certainly, the general feeling locally was that the harbour was poorly managed.

Matters did improve, however, when the second Earl of Stradbroke, John Edward Cornwallis Rous, inherited the title on his father's death in August 1827. He was a Rous with nous having served as an officer under the tutelage of Wellington. One look at the Harbour Commission and the dire state of the harbour itself was enough to make him realise a radical overhaul of its management was required and he took up the challenge. This was not a merely philanthropic gesture - he needed the harbour to function properly in order to ship in building materials for Henham Hall and coal supplies for the estate, and to ship out his corn and other estate produce, but his efforts to introduce professional management paid dividends for the town also. Sir John gave his time to the town in other ways as well, serving as a magistrate. As Rachel Lawrence says in her book *Southwold River* "John Edward Cornwallis Rous, second Lord of Stradbroke, was the natural leader in the Blyth Valley and accepted as such without question by a community which believed that ownership of land gave an inalienable right to lead and dictate. Stradbroke saw it as a right and a duty".

If he had seen it solely as a right then changing St James Street to Stradbroke Road may indeed have been corporate fawning but as he saw it as a duty it was an entirely reasonable recognition of his contribution to the town's well-being, especially as the Corporation did not agree to change the name until after his death in 1886.

STRICKLAND PLACE

Strickland Place was named after the Victorian writer Agnes Strickland, who is remembered primarily for her *Lives of the Queens of England* which she co-wrote with her less forceful sister, Eliza.

Agnes would have relished having a road named after her, holding herself as she did, in great esteem - she recorded once that " it is with the higher circles I feel most at ease" -

but she might have been disappointed by the size of Strickland Place given the length of highway devoted to her fellow historian, Thomas Gardner.

The Strickland family of six sisters and one brother was brought up in Reydon Hall. Agnes' sister Jane bought Park Lane Cottage (now Strickland House) in the early 1850s as a bolt-hole from the incessant pressures of being the prime carer for the widowed Mrs Strickland. Agnes spent much of her time in London where she moved in high circles as a result of the popularity of her histories. However, when Mrs Strickland died Reydon Hall was sold and in 1865 Agnes decided to move to Southwold, leasing Park Lane Cottage from Jane, a somewhat curious arrangement whereby Agnes lived in the main building and Jane, the ostensible owner of the house, was shunted into the annexe. If they argued, the connecting door between the two was locked.

Agnes died in Park Lane Cottage in 1874. This was just the time when the Council decided to let six building plots nearby at the edge of The Common on 75 year building leases. It might be assumed that the Council thought then that it would be appropriate to honour the lady whose grave in St Edmund's churchyard bears the inscription "Historian of the Queens of England" and who had lived nearby, but that was not, in fact, the case. It was not until the 1911 meeting that the Council resolved that the stretch from "Daisy Villa to Godyll Road" be named Strickland Place (Daisy Villa being the property at the Woodley's Yard end of Gardner Road now called Hillcrest - the original name can just be seen through subsequent layers of paint) and it was an even longer wait before the name appeared on the electoral rolls - 1946. By then Agnes' glories had somewhat faded from the universal consciousness but Park Lane Cottage had become the home of that equally redoubtable woman, Fanny Foster (see Foster Close). She was a member of the Borough Council by that time and in a perfect position to champion Agnes and ensure that her name, if not her reputation, endured.

TIBBY'S GREEN AND TIBBY'S WAY

Here we enter a spelling controversy. Tibby was the local name for an unweaned calf and tibbies stayed in what was still a field here until they were old enough to fend for themselves on The Common. Given that undoubtedly more than one calf resided here at any one time the logical way of spelling the name of this green would be Tibbies but there was uproar when the Southwold & Reydon Society did precisely that when they presented signs for all the town's greens to mark the Millennium and so the sign had to be re-done and Tibby's it was. Tibby's Way is the roadway on the former Distribution Centre development leading from Victoria Street to Field Stile Road and of the three street names on the development, the only one which has not caused comment.

TRINITY STREET

Trinity Street was called Green Lane until a Council resolution of 3rd February 1871. A green lane was traditionally a grassy way across farmland and on the 17th century map the route of this lane passes alongside the land of Pinkneys Farm towards the pastureland beyond. It is possible too that it was called Green Lane because it went in the direction of Little East Green as it is marked on the 1801 Ablett's map (now East Cliff). Green Lane probably did not seem appropriate when farmland gave way to housing. Why Trinity Street? I can only assume it was because of the historical importance to the town of the Trinity as reflected in the Holy Trinity Chapel in the church and its Trinity Fair held since 1489 but now called Charter Fair.

VICTORIA STREET

Victoria Street, the road of many names. In the 1801 Ablett map its whole length is marked as East Lane. By 1839 Wake indicates that the easterly end from the present Trinity Street to East Green was called East Lane, that the stretch from East Green to Bartholomew Green was Back Street and that from Bartholomew Green to the High Street the road was called Camels Lane. At that time the road continued in a straight line before it joined the High Street, with cottages on either side. Those on the Electricity Green side were demolished to widen the junction. Thomas Camel was a bailiff of the town who lived in a house in that area.

On occasions the East Green to Trinity Street section has also been called Tape Street. By 1884, however, the Ordnance Survey map shows the whole length being called Victoria Street. A loyal gesture, no doubt. Southwold was clearly fond of Queen Victoria. On 10th February 1840 a public dinner was held to mark her wedding and in 1842 the guns on Gun Hill were fired in her honour as she sailed by on her way to Scotland. Maggs records that Victoria sailed by Southwold again on 6th September 1848 although he does not record a further loyal salute. Sufficient evidence, though, to indicate that the town shared the nation's feelings about its monarch and to explain the naming of the road.

WOODLEY'S YARD

Woodley's Yard has to be one of the coldest places in Southwold and you have to be really short of readies to queue at the cash machine there when the wind blows. It was not always Woodley's Yard of course. It is marked merely as Backway on the mid 19th century map but the land immediately south of it was identified as belonging to Mr Crisp. William Crisp was a brewer and maltster whose home was where Barclays now stands and who called his brewery the Home Maltings. Bernard Segrave-Daly recalls in his chapter on Brewing and Pubs in *Southwold: Portraits of an English Seaside Town*, that the site of the present United Reformed Church was the brewery yard and that William Crisp sold the Home Maltings to John Banham Woodley in 1866.

There was another Woodley associated with Southwold and with brewing. William Matthew Woodley was a councillor who topped the polls in 1847 with 56 votes. He also joined forces with Samuel Gayfer, a Walberswick businessman, to form Gayfer & Woodley, brewers and merchants, but they did not operate from the present Woodleys Yard; Council Minutes from 1844 recording the organisation of Beating the Bounds refer to the "buying of a barrel of beer from Gayfer & Woodley's East Green Brewery". No, it was John Banham Woodley after whom the pathway was named. Until 1881 there was an archway over the High Street entrance to Woodley's Yard which would once have been the main entrance to the bustling brewery yard and the brewer's home. Council Minutes record that in December 1913 the then owners of Woodley's Yard asked for a footpath to be formed between the High Street and The Common. Permission was granted and the Council contributed a third of the cost.

WYMERING ROAD

Wymering Road has made me feel a failure. Clearly it was called Wymering Road because at least part of it was built on land formerly belonging to Wymering House, 47 High Street, but why Wymering? It derives from the Saxon Wygmaer ingas which means the people of Wygmaer - and that does not get us very far. There is, however, a Wymering near Portsmouth. There was a Roman settlement at Wymering between roughly 43 and 408AD and the Domesday Book refers to 'the manor house of Wymering' which is recorded in 1042 as belonging to Edward the Confessor and, after the Battle of Hastings, as becoming the property of William the Conqueror.

But wait, all is not lost. The 1809 Ablett Map shows a tranche of land abutting the High Street in the area of Wymering House which is marked as belonging to a Mrs Revans. The wonders of Wikipedia threw up the existence of a Professor Reginald William Revans, born in 1907 near Portsmouth. Perhaps Mrs Revans herself hailed from those parts and was young Reg's aunt

The Church of the Sacred Heart, Wymering Road

YORK ROAD

York Road was part of the late Victorian West End Development (see Manor Park Road). On the 1839 map it is shown as a track beginning at Barnaby Green and leading across The Common to "Blackshore and the Lime Kiln" and as late as 1891 it is still thus marked albeit without reference to a lime kiln. It was at the, by now, much-mentioned 1911 meeting of the Corporation that it was proposed that the stretch "between the north Common gate and Anchor Villa" be called York Road.

The north Common gate was near the junction with Godyll Road, where the royal trees are, and Anchor Villa was, as noted under Station Road, the name of the private house at the junction of Blackmill Road and the High Street now occupied by Fat Face. York Road first features in the municipal rolls in 1913.

So, that's where and when, but why? Southwold has had associations with several people bearing the name or title of York. For a time in the 14th - 15th centuries the town was in the possession of Richard, Earl of Cambridge, who was executed for treason by Henry V in 1415. His estate then passed to his son, Richard, Duke of York, who led the Yorkists at the beginning of the Wars of the Roses. He too was executed, in 1460, but in the 1450s had had the foresight to convey at least the Southwold part of his estate to trustees acting on behalf of his son who in due course became Edward IV. Twenty nine years later, Henry VII granted Southwold its first Charter and Henry's wife was Elizabeth of York. However, significant as those connections are, the Corporation probably had in mind the more vivid association of the Duke of York and the Battle of Sole Bay in 1672 during which the ill-fated Earl of Sandwich set up campaign headquarters in Sutherland House and where the latter is reputed to have dallied with a servant girl whose ghost still haunts the place awaiting his return.

The same Duke of York, forgetting Southwold's earlier hospitality, decided in 1685 to call in the 1489 Charter and issue a new, more prescriptive document which severely cut back the local democracy enjoyed by the town for the previous 200 years. This document became known as 'the Usurping Charter' and, thankfully, was in turn rescinded in 1690, during the reign of William and Mary, and the old Charter reissued and confirmed.

York Road, looking towards the Water Towers

Maybe the Corporation in 1911 was seduced by the 'romance' of the battle of Sole Bay and had forgotten the subsequent effrontery of the Usurping Charter; William and Mary Road would have been more justified if less snappy. As luck would have it, though, the Corporation seemed to have had a certain prescience here as York Road did subsequently seem entirely appropriate when between 1931 and 1939 the tents and marquees of the then Duke of York's Camps sprang up annually on The Common a step or two beyond York Road. Did he notice the road name, that Duke of York, soon to be a reluctant king? Did he wonder if the Council had moved with unaccustomed speed to honour him? They had not, of course, but he was, perhaps, as worthy of recognition as his predecessors so it was something of a happy accident.

YOUNGS YARD

I like to think that Youngs Yard was named after the Reverend Christopher Yonges who died on 14th June 1626 and who is interred in the church, or after his eldest son, John Yonges, who founded Southwold's daughter town, Southold on Long Island, New York. John was a minister himself and lived in Southwold during his early years and the Southwold register records the baptism of two of his children. He appears to have left England with his family in 1637, settling first in Salem, Massachusetts, and then Newhaven, Connecticut, before moving to Long Island. One imagines that correspondence between Southold and Southwold would have been almost impossible in those early years but a connection was maintained which persists to this day and which may account for the apparently anomalous names given to parts of the sea front: Long Island Cliff,

New York Cliff, California and the Klondyke. The proximity of Youngs Yard to the church would seem to support the connection with the 17th century Youngs. However, wishing does not make it so.

Roads were unnamed in the 17th century and there were later families of that name in town. Maggs notes that in 1846 on "Sep 6th Revd Mr Young commenced his Curacy here". He did not hang around long enough to have even a small cul-de-sac named after him, however, Maggs recording that the following year on "Sep 26 Revd Mr Young preaches his farewell Sermon. 29th left ye Curacy." Less than a fortnight later Rev John Henry Young late of Southwold is recorded as marrying in London.

There are other Youngs though : Maggs refers to the assignment in 1852 of the goods of Henry Youngs, draper and grocer of Somerleyton and in 1870 to, presumably, another Henry Youngs who hired the Brick Kiln from the Corporation in 1870. And the final nail in the coffin of the romantic American connection - White's 1870 Suffolk Directory records the residence in Victoria Street of Henry Youngs, beerhouse owner and corn chandler. His home was the property later called The Royal which was subsequently for many years, until his death in 2010, the home of the bandleader, Jack Parnell. Youngs Yard is not directly opposite The Royal but near enough to suggest that Henry Youngs used it as his yard. But if you see any of our Southold visitors having their photographs taken in front of the Youngs Yard sign, be kind and don't disabuse them!